Crunch Time

Facing the Crisis of Life

By

Dr. R. B. Ouellette

SWORD of the LORD PUBLISHERS

Post Office Box 1099 • Murfreesboro, Tennessee 37133

All Scripture quotations are from
the King James Bible.

Printed and Bound in the United States of America

Contents

Dedication

This book is dedicated with love to our daughter Karissa and her husband, Thomas Coats. It is a daily delight to serve the Lord together with you both. I love you.

Acknowledgments

I am again indebted to Brother Robert Byers, who transcribed this material, deleted that which was extraneous and made many helpful contributions and suggestions. I also wish to thank Brother Guy King for his work in layout and design and Dr. Shelton Smith for his kindness in allowing this book to be published. Thanks to Andy Ash for doing such a great job designing this cover as well as the covers for *Living in an Imperfect World* and *Things That Aren't So*.

Most important, I wish to thank my lovely wife Krisy for over a third of a century of love and support. I love you, Sweetheart.

1

Grief

Grief is a universal condition of the human race. Ever since sin entered into the world through Adam, we have been subject to pain, broken hearts and death. Sometimes I run into a "really spiritual" person who thinks that grief is wrong. Yet the Bible calls Jesus "a man of sorrows, and acquainted with grief."

The Bible never says that Christians don't grieve or have sorrow. It does say that we "sorrow not, even as others which have no hope" (I Thess. 4:13). The difference is not in avoiding grief, but in how we deal with things that come into our lives and cause us pain.

A lady I did not know called me one time and asked me to pray for her son. He had been diagnosed with a brain tumor. He was just sixteen years old, but he had only a short time to live. She said, "O Lord, no! Take me and let my son live." I prayed with her and tried to help her, but I didn't quite know what to say in the face of such grief.

Not everyone responds the same way to grief, but everybody who loves someone grieves when they lose that loved one.

Examples of Grief

1. Examples From the Word

Samuel grieved when Saul backslid.

> *"Then came the word of the LORD unto Samuel, saying,*
>
> *"It repenteth me that I have set up Saul to be king: for he is turned back from following me, and hath not performed my commandments. And it grieved Samuel; and he cried unto the LORD all night."*—I Sam. 15:10, 11.

When somebody who is in a position of leadership falls away from God, it is not an occasion to criticize. The first reaction of many people is to pick up the telephone and spread the news. Instead it should cause us to grieve. Samuel could have responded differently. Until Saul became king, Samuel was the highest authority in Israel under God. He was the prophet and judge over the people.

But the people told Samuel that because he was old and his sons did not follow his ways, they wanted a king. Samuel made the same tragic mistake Eli did in serving God himself but failing to teach his children to love and obey God. So he anointed Saul to lead the nation. He could have responded to Saul's failure by saying, "I told you so." He could have viewed it as vindication, but instead it broke his heart.

Jacob grieved over the loss of Joseph.

> *"And Jacob rent his clothes, and put sackcloth upon his loins, and mourned for his son many days.*
>
> *"And all his sons and all his daughters rose up to comfort him; but he refused to be comforted; and he said, For I will go down into the grave unto my son mourning. Thus his father wept for him."*—Gen. 37:34, 35.

Joseph's brothers got to the point where they were sick and tired of the favoritism Jacob showed Joseph. So when they had the opportunity, they sold him into slavery. To cover up their evil deed, they took Joseph's coat of many colors, dipped it in blood and told Jacob they had found it. He recognized it as Joseph's coat and, as they had intended, believed his favored son was dead.

In Bible times people did not have many clothes like we do today. They were much harder to make, and even a wealthy man like Jacob probably only had a few garments. So it was a sign of tremendous grief for a person to rend his garments. Jacob then put on sackcloth, which was very uncomfortable to wear. But he wore it as an outward sign of the inward grief he was feeling in his spirit.

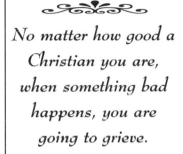

No matter how good a Christian you are, when something bad happens, you are going to grieve.

The typical mourning period lasted seven days. People would stay inside their homes and not even put on their shoes, because they had no plans to go out. It was an expression of their grief over the loss of a loved one. Jacob grieved for the loss of Joseph for "many days."

Job and his friends grieved over the loss of his family and possessions.

"*Now when Job's three friends heard of all this evil that was come upon him, they came every one from his own place; Eliphaz the Temanite, and Bildad the Shuhite, and Zophar the Naamathite: for they had made an appointment together to come to mourn with him and to comfort him.*

"And when they lifted up their eyes afar off, and knew him not, they lifted up their voice, and wept; and they rent every one his mantle, and sprinkled dust upon their heads toward heaven.

"So they sat down with him upon the ground seven days

and seven nights, and none spake a word unto him: for they saw that his grief was very great."—Job 2:11–13.

When you go to see someone who is grieving, your presence will often bring more comfort than your words would. In fact, when Job's friends started talking, things started going downhill! Not every silence or empty space has to be filled with words. There is a great comfort to the grieving just from your presence. Often when people don't know what to say, they end up saying something that isn't well thought-out or supported by Scripture. Just be there.

David mourned for Saul and Jonathan.

"Then David took hold on his clothes, and rent them; and likewise all the men that were with him:

"And they mourned, and wept, and fasted until even, for Saul, and for Jonathan his son, and for the people of the LORD, and for the house of Israel; because they were fallen by the sword."—II Sam. 1:11, 12.

Saul was David's enemy, but David refused to be an enemy of Saul. Even though Saul tried to kill David repeatedly, David chose not to kill Saul on two separate occasions when he had opportunity to do so. Saul had caused David to flee his home and live in the wilderness. But when Saul died, David did not express relief or joy. We would no doubt have excused him if he had said, "God has finally vindicated me and judged Saul. I knew this would happen because of how he acted toward me." But he did not.

Though David had suffered at the hand of Saul, there had also been good things in his relationship with Saul. The shepherd from the backwoods had been given the opportunity to learn the ways of ruling in the palace by living with Saul and watching him rule. Rather than focusing on the bad, David remembered the good that Saul had done, both for Israel and for him personally.

David mourned over Absalom.

"And the king said unto Cushi, Is the young man Absalom safe? And Cushi answered, The enemies of my lord the king, and all that rise against thee to do thee hurt, be as that young man is.

"And the king was much moved, and went up to the chamber over the gate, and wept: and as he went, thus he said, O my son Absalom, my son, my son Absalom! would God I had died for thee, O Absalom, my son, my son!"—II Sam. 18:32, 33.

I think in all of Scripture this may be the passage filled with the most emotion and pathos. When David heard the news that Absalom had lost his life, his heart was broken. Even though Absalom had rebelled against him and driven him from Jerusalem, David would have traded his own life for that of his son.

2. Examples From the World

As I tell the people at our church, whenever we look at something that does not have the authority of Scripture, we do not have to believe it. But a number of people have spent time analyzing grief, and in their observations about grief and how people respond to it, there are things that are helpful to us as we go through painful experiences.

Elisabeth Kubler-Ross wrote a book called *On Death and Dying* in 1969. By citing this book, I am by no means endorsing all of her writings or ideas. Especially later in her life, she became involved in some very strange beliefs, including working extensively with mediums. But her early books were based on her scholarship (she had a Ph.D. in psychiatry and also was an M.D.) and contain some helpful material.

On Death and Dying describes five stages of the grieving process based on Kubler-Ross' observation and experience working with the terminally ill. Not everyone goes through all five stages, and not everyone has them in the same order. Nor are they necessarily separate stages; people often experience more than one of them at the same time. But they are emotions and thoughts that are very common among the grieving.

Denial. I knew a person who was terminally ill, and everyone knew it except for one of the family members. That person kept behaving like nothing was wrong and everything was going to be just fine. That one person simply refused to accept the facts that were plainly obvious to everyone else. I am not talking about people who have prayed and have faith for healing; I'm talking about people who are not dealing with reality.

Anger. Many times people feel what has happened to them is not fair. And, of course, many things that are unjust and painful do happen because we live in a sinful world. Often this anger turns against God. During the Tribulation, men will curse the name of God because of the torments they are enduring (Rev. 16:21).

Bargaining. We sometimes try to make deals with God to get us out of trouble when we're in distress. That's how Martin Luther became a monk. He was so scared by being caught out in a thunderstorm that he promised to join the priesthood if he survived. Of course the Catholic Church probably isn't too glad he kept his side of the bargain!

Depression. Eventually most people reach the point of resignation. They've basically given up. They're no longer trying to find a way out of their situation, nor do they have the strength left to be angry. The reality of the situation has fully sunk in, and they are tired and discouraged.

Acceptance. Jeremiah reached this point. He said, "Truly this is a grief, and I must bear it" (Jer. 10:19). He did not diminish the reality of the situation, nor did he try to escape it. He simply realized that his grief was what God had for him at that moment in his life and he would have to deal with the pain of his situation.

Dr. Roberta Temes, in her book *Living With an Empty Chair,* used a somewhat different classification. I strongly disagree with her emphasis on hypnosis as a means of healing, but there is material in her book that I think is useful in understanding grief. She described three phases that people go through.

Numbness. At this stage people function mechanically. They are going through the motions of life. Social interactions are very much limited to the surface level. It is as if they are insulated from the people with whom they come in contact, even those who are closest to them.

Disorganization. The person feels intense feelings of loss. Often they withdraw from the routines of life. They may gain or lose a large amount of weight, or they may begin destructive behaviors such as drinking, drugs or immorality. Life seems to be out of control because of the pain they are feeling.

Reorganization. This is where the person's life begins to come back together. They recognize the depth of the loss but also begin to move forward. Normal sleep and appetite patterns return, and they begin to go for longer and longer periods of time without focusing on the loss they have suffered.

Explanation of Grief

1. Definition of Grief

Grief is an outward expression of an inward emotion. It is simply showing on the outside what you are feeling within. The Bible words used for grief mean "to sorrow, to suffer loss, to feel pain, to bewail, or to be angry." No matter how good a Christian you are, when something sad happens, you are going to grieve.

2. Demonstration of Grief

Grief demonstrates some things in your life. Not everyone will express his grief in the same way that you do, but that does not mean that he cares less than you do about the person or situation. Even when people express their grief differently, their grief still demonstrates some things.

Love. While the war in Iraq has been going on, we've often heard of soldiers who have been killed. Every time I hear that a brave man or woman has died in the service of our country, I feel bad about that. They are making an enormous sacrifice on our behalf.

Still, I don't feel nearly as bad as I would if it was Troy Richard who was in one of those bombings, because I know him and love him. I pray for him everyday. I try to help his wife and look out for his children, and I look forward to the time he comes home for good.

At the tomb where Lazarus was buried, just before He raised Lazarus from the dead, Jesus wept. What did those who saw Him weeping say? "Behold how he loved him!" (John 11:36). Jesus' outward expression of grief was a demonstration of His love for His friend.

> *It is completely right and appropriate to grieve when we suffer loss.*

Loss. While I was preparing this message, a dear man in our church lost his wife. When I got the news and went to see him, he was composed. He was not totally distraught or running around the house saying crazy things. But his deep grief was evident on his face.

He said to me, "I don't want her to be gone. I just miss her.

I wish I still had her." They were just one month short of their 58th wedding anniversary. He said "I didn't want it to be like this." I said, "What did you want?" He said "I just wanted us to keep on going. I told her we had to go for seventy-five— you know, get on Paul Harvey maybe." His pain showed the depth of the loss he had suffered.

Life. Did you know the fact that you can grieve proves that you have a soul? I think animals can miss a master that they're close to or a mate that they had for a long time, but animals don't cry. You never have to say to someone, "Be nice to that doggy; don't make it cry." They whimper, they bark, they make noise, they express pain, but animals don't cry, because animals don't have souls.

Animals ought to be treated kindly (Prov. 12:10). I don't believe in cruelty to animals, but God made them for us. If you grieve, that is evidence that you have a soul. Grief demonstrates life.

Exhortations About Grief

1. The Propriety of Grief

Despite what some really pious people say, it is completely right and appropriate to grieve when things happen in our lives that are painful. Solomon wrote:

"To every thing there is a season, and a time to every purpose under the heaven:

"A time to be born, and a time to die; a time to plant, and a time to pluck up that which is planted;

"A time to kill, and a time to heal; a time to break down, and a time to build up;

"A time to weep, and a time to laugh; a time to mourn, and a time to dance."—Eccles. 3:1–4.

The Bible says that there is a time when it is fitting and

appropriate for us to weep or to mourn. David knew what it was like to suffer. He wrote, "Thou tellest my wanderings: put thou my tears into thy bottle: are they not in thy book?" (Ps. 56:8).

In Bible times many people had a little jar called a lachrymatory. It was usually made of clay. They used it to collect their tears as an expression of their sadness or mourning. Sometimes they would bury that jar of tears with or near their loved one or place it upon their grave. They thought their evidences of grief were significant enough to be kept as a remembrance.

In fact, such tear bottles were still used into Victorian times. In England, the tears for a dead loved one would be captured in a bottle. When all the tears had evaporated, the official mourning period would be considered over.

The title of Psalm 56 tells us that it is a song David wrote when he was hiding from Saul among the Philistines in Gath. Certainly he had much over which to mourn in those days. The psalmist said to God, "I am weeping and crying, but I am not collecting the tears. Will you please collect them for me?" In effect David was saying, "God, please notice that I'm hurting."

As a matter of fact, it is so appropriate to grieve that when God wants somebody not to grieve, it's a rare and unusual thing. God had Ezekiel do many strange things as signs to the nation of Israel, but one of the more remarkable ones involved his wife. Ezekiel loved his wife dearly; she was "the desire of [his] eyes." Yet, when she died suddenly, God told him not to mourn for her.

> *"Son of man, behold, I take away from thee the desire of thine eyes with a stroke: yet neither shalt thou mourn nor weep, neither shall thy tears run down.*
>
> *"Forbear to cry, make no mourning for the dead, bind the tire of thine head upon thee, and put on thy shoes upon thy*

feet, and cover not thy lips, and eat not the bread of men. *"So I spake unto the people in the morning: and at even my wife died; and I did in the morning as I was commanded."*—Ezek. 24:16–18.

This was not normal behavior. In fact, the people came to Ezekiel and wanted to know why he was behaving in such an unusual manner (Ezek. 24:19). God didn't have to command someone to grieve; it was so normal to grieve that He had to command Ezekiel not to grieve.

2. The Purpose of Grief

The process of grieving is not just a time of sadness. It also can serve valuable purposes in our lives.

One of the primary purposes of grief is to express. Grief expresses emotion, it expresses love, and it expresses loss.

I remember hearing Dr. Jack Hyles tell about a little bus girl who came to his church. She called him Mr. Brother Hyles. When she would see him, see would say, "Mr. Brother Hyles, you're my best friend." He would reply, "Thank you, Sweetie. I love you and I appreciate you."

One day she came in and sadly said, "Mr. Brother Hyles, I'm not going to come here anymore. My family's moving.

> *The expression of grief allows us to process the emotions that we are feeling.*

I'm going to live someplace too far away to come to the church." He said "I'm sorry, Sweetheart." She said, "Mr. Brother Hyles, I won't ever be here again. I'm moving away." He said again, "I'm sure sorry you're not going to come here."

She said, "Mr. Brother Hyles, you're my best friend, and I'm leaving, and I'll never see you again." He said "Honey, I'm sure sorry about that. We'll really miss you." She looked up at him and said "Mr. Brother Hyles, ain't you gonna cry?"

Expressing our grief allows us to process the emotions that we feel.

Don't be afraid or ashamed to cry if you need to. Don't be afraid to be sad if you need to. Don't feel like expressing grief somehow makes you ungodly or unspiritual. David grieved, and he was a man after God's own heart. Samuel, who was God's prophet and priest and the judge of Israel, grieved over Saul.

Another purpose of grief is to eliminate. Grieving lets out the emotions and in the process helps us move on past them. Now men don't understand this as much, but I've had ladies say to me, "I just needed to have a good cry." After they cry, they feel better.

After someone expresses his emotions and has let some of them out, he often feels like things have improved. An expression of grief does not totally rid us of sorrow, but by venting, we eliminate some sorrow and let it out. On the side of the tires on my car, there is a warning against over-inflating. A buildup of excess pressure can be dangerous— not just to tires, but to people also. Grieving allows you to release some of the pressure you are feeling because of the loss you have suffered.

3. The Product of Grief

It's interesting to me that different people can go different directions when they grieve. Some may ask whether grief is good or bad for a person, and the answer is that it depends on the person's response. There are some people who respond to their sadness and hardship by becoming closer to God. As a result of what they have been through, they have a tenderer heart, a more open spirit and a willingness to help those around them.

Grief can produce bitterness. While some respond properly, there are others who respond to their grief by getting angry and upset and turning *from* God instead of *toward* God. We see an example of this in the Book of Ruth. Naomi, along with her husband and her two sons, went to Moab because of a famine in Israel. Now that was not the right thing to do. I believe it shows a lack of faith and confidence in God. But that was the decision that they made.

While they were in Moab, Naomi's sons met and married girls from Moab. (That's one of the reasons it was wrong for them to go there—God does not want His children marrying heathens.) Over the course

> *Bitterness is produced when people who in their grief turn from God rather than to God.*

of time, both sons and her husband died. When Naomi decided to return to Bethlehem, she urged her daughters-in-law to remain behind. Orpah agreed, but Ruth refused and insisted on accompanying Naomi back to Israel. Notice Naomi's response to the people when she returned:

"And she said unto them, Call me not Naomi, call me Mara: for the Almighty hath dealt very bitterly with me.

"I went out full, and the LORD hath brought me home again empty: why then call ye me Naomi, seeing the LORD hath testified against me, and the Almighty hath afflicted me?"—Ruth 1:20, 21.

Bitterness over her grief had totally warped Naomi's perspective. She said that she went out full, but, in fact, they left because of a famine. She said that she came back empty, but she was accompanied by the loyal and loving Ruth. By the end of the Book of Ruth, we see Naomi happy again, but her first response to grief was the wrong response.

Grief can produce bad behavior. First Samuel 30 gives us a story from the life of David that shows how grief can lead

13

people to act wrongly. David was at Ziklag, and it was a downtime in his career. It was a negative experience and a low point in his life. I have heard people preach on this chapter and say that David had to go through his experiences at Ziklag to get to the throne and that you are going to have to go through Ziklag experiences if you are going to get to your throne.

There is an element of truth to what they say. There are indeed many valleys through which we travel on our way to the mountaintop. But David never should have been at Ziklag in the first place. David was in Ziklag because when he was running from Saul, he had hooked up with the Philistines and become a liar.

He would tell Achish, the king of Gath, that he had been out to battle against the Israelites (I Sam. 27:10). He really wasn't doing that. He was fighting against common enemies of the Philistines and Israelites. But he wanted Achish to think that he was totally against Israel and totally on the side of this Philistine king. And do you know what David did to preserve his deception? He killed everybody he fought—not only the men, but also the women, "lest they should tell on us" (I Sam. 27:11).

This was not a very godly time in David's life. He wasn't trusting God. David didn't need to worry about being killed by Saul. There was not one chance in the world that Saul was going to succeed in killing David. David had been anointed by Samuel as God's choice to sit on Israel's throne.

David could have said, "Saul can hunt me with 3,000 men or 300,000 men; he can throw three javelins at me or thirty javelins at me. God said I am going to be the next king of Israel, and they never put a dead man on the throne." David didn't have anything to worry about.

But instead of trusting God, he ran away. As a result, he lied and killed innocent people. One day when David and his men went off to battle, they returned to find their wives and children gone and the entire city burned to the ground. The Bible says they wept until they had no more power to weep. As a result of their anger over what they had lost, the men began to discuss stoning David (I Sam. 30:6).

They said, "We wouldn't be in this mess if we hadn't followed David. We had a decent home where we lived before. We followed this guy thinking that he was something special. He led us to believe there was some great plan for the future, and now look at the mess he's gotten us into."

Grief can make people turn on God or get angry at God's people. Rather than seeking out fellowship in the church when they're in grief, they pull away and leave the principles of a lifetime. I've heard people say, "I've been trying to do right, I've been faithful to church, I've been reading my Bible and giving generously, and now look what's happened to me. Why even bother? I might as well just give it all up."

Grief can produce blessing. You might ask, what blessing is there in grief?

The blessing of comfort. Jesus said, "Blessed are they that mourn: for they shall be comforted" (Matt. 5:4).

From whom do you receive comfort? You may well get it from family or from friends, but you certainly get it from your Father in Heaven, because He is the God of all comfort (II Cor. 1:3). I love the song that says:

**When no one cared about me, if I should live or die,
And no one bothered asking why I'd go alone and cry;
When burdens got so heavy I couldn't face the day,
Then I'd feel His arm around me, and I'd hear
    Him gently say,**

**"Lean on me when you have no strength to stand;
When you feel you're going under, hold tighter to My hand.
Lean on me when your heart begins to bleed;**

**When you come to the place where I'm all you've got,
Then you'll find I'm all you need."**

You learn to know the Shepherd better in the valley than you do on the mountaintop. There is a sweetness that comes in the presence of God in a time of burden and hardship that never seems to come in a time of victory and success. You will never know how much some people care or how interested they are until your troubles come.

The blessing of companionship. Jesus said,

> *"Blessed are ye, when men shall revile you, and persecute you, and shall say all manner of evil against you falsely, for my sake.*
>
> *"Rejoice, and be exceeding glad: for great is your reward in heaven: for so persecuted they the prophets which were before you."*—Matt. 5:11, 12.

When you are hurting, it's important to remember that you are not alone.

We often refer to Hebrews 11, the great faith chapter of the Bible, as God's Hall of Faith. We read about Moses, Abraham, Enoch, Abel, Joshua and Rahab. All of these heroes of the faith endured hardship and difficulty. And I believe that God tells us their stories to remind us that other folks have been through the same troubles we're going through. You're not the first person to be betrayed by a loved one, to be abandoned by your friends, to suffer a terrible affliction or to lose all your financial resources.

Remember others who have suffered. If people treat you a little bit like they did Paul and Peter, you're in pretty good company. If they reject you like they did Jesus, if they attack you and criticize you like they did Moses, you're not in bad shape. You are not alone, because the Spirit of God is with you. You are also not alone, because other people have been there before you.

16

4. Some Precautions About Grief

Hebrews 13:17 says, "Obey them that have the rule over you, and submit yourselves: for they watch for your souls, as they that must give account, that they may do it with joy, and not with grief: for that is unprofitable for you." If you don't follow the spiritual leadership that God has placed in your life, it will cause grief and will be unprofitable for you.

The truth is that a lot of the grief in this world is self-inflicted. When we fail to obey authority, we are setting ourselves up to suffer. Many times I have counseled people who were in tears in my office over something that had happened. And many of those times, it is

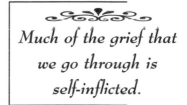

Much of the grief that we go through is self-inflicted.

because they have rejected the principles of the Word of God that I have preached from the pulpit. Obey authority, and you will avoid a lot of grief.

Another precaution about grief is found in Proverbs 5:11, 12:

"And thou mourn at the last, when thy flesh and thy body are consumed,

"And say, How have I hated instruction, and my heart despised reproof."

These verses are found in a passage warning against the dangers of immorality. But there is a larger principle at work here: Going off in the wrong direction and yielding to the Devil's temptation brings you mourning; it brings you grief.

We see another warning about grief in the prayer of Jabez (I Chron. 4:9, 10). First, he prayed that he might be more productive. Then he prayed that God would give him power. Finally, he prayed for protection from evil "that it may not grieve me!" Jabez realized that in the midst of blessing and great spiritual increase and enjoying the power of God in his life, he could still go off into evil. Great spiritual blessing, great success in the work of God does not guarantee you victory against temptation.

5. The Plan for Grief

We must accept grief.

Jeremiah 10:19 says, "Truly this is a grief, and I must bear it." I may not like grief, but I cannot escape it. I can't avoid it, and I can't pretend it's not there; I must bear it. Grief is a universal reality of our fallen world.

> *"And he said unto me, My grace is sufficient for thee: for my strength is made perfect in weakness. Most gladly therefore will I rather glory in my infirmities, that the power of Christ may rest upon me.*
>
> *"Therefore I take pleasure in infirmities, in reproaches, in necessities, in persecutions, in distresses for Christ's sake: for when I am weak, then am I strong."*—II Cor. 12:9, 10.

Paul is talking here about his thorn in the flesh. He begged God three times to remove it from him, and this was God's answer. I do not like all the things that God brings into my life, but I must accept them. The only way that we can do this is through the grace of God.

We must ask for help.

> *"I will call upon the LORD, who is worthy to be praised: so shall I be saved from mine enemies."*
>
> *"In my distress I called upon the LORD, and cried unto my God: he heard my voice out of his temple, and my cry came before him, even into his ears."*—Ps. 18:3, 6.

This is a Psalm that David wrote to celebrate God's delivering him from King Saul.

David was in great danger. Yet instead of complaining,

he called on the Lord. When you're in trouble, when you're going through a time of grief, don't run *from* God; run *to* God. Don't drift *away* from God; get closer *to* God. When you feel you're going under, hold tighter to his hand. God makes a place of protection for us as His children. It is up to us to ask for His help when we are hurting and in need.

I heard about a painting that showed a raging fire in the forest and a group of animals running toward an ark. (I'm not sure why the artist chose to show a fire with the ark instead of a flood, but that's what he did.) The title of the painting was *Refuge*. God is always faithful; run to Him and seek His help. He will grant you comfort from every grief that you have to bear.

"Trust in him at all times; ye people, pour out your heart before him: God is a refuge for us."—Ps. 62:8.

2

Temptation

What do you do when temptation comes? You can be certain that it will. The Bible says, "Be sober, be vigilant; because your adversary the devil, as a roaring lion, walketh about, seeking whom he may devour" (I Pet. 5:8). How can you survive his attacks?

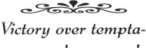

Victory over temptation is determined before it ever comes.

Let me suggest to you that the time to decide what to do is not when the temptation comes. You need to decide ahead of time how you will react, if you want to have any hope of making the right decision when the temptation comes. A young man and his girlfriend are out together sitting by the river with moonbeams striking the water and the fireflies flickering around. The scent of her perfume fills his nostrils. At that moment the tempter says, "Kiss her."

It is highly unlikely that he will remember a single Bible verse at a time like that! He will not be disposed to contemplate the other covenants, promises and commitments he has made. That's not the time to decide. He needs to decide beforehand. In fact, I tell our young people that it's a good idea to establish their standards before they begin dating.

There's probably not a better illustration of the process of temptation and the response to it in all of Scripture than the story of Joseph. When faced with a great temptation to sin, he fled. How did Joseph do right? Let's examine the story.

The Setting Appreciated

We need to understand the conditions that were in place when Joseph faced his temptation. It didn't just arise out of thin air; there was a long series of circumstances that led to Joseph's being where he was. Those circumstances potentially could have influenced his response.

1. Joseph Was Betrayed

Joseph would never have been in Egypt had it not been for the betrayal of his brothers. They were jealous of the fact that Joseph was their father's favorite son. The coat of many colors was a symbol that he did not have to do the same kind of manual labor that they did. On top of that, Joseph's dreams revealed that God was going to bless him and give him a position of authority over them.

The Bible says to weep with those who weep and to rejoice with those who rejoice (Rom. 12:15). But I've observed that for most people it's easier to share sorrows and burdens than truly to rejoice with others over their blessings. We tend to be jealous instead of grateful for blessings of others. Joseph's brothers weren't at all excited about the prospect of his being elevated by God. Things got even worse when Joseph told Jacob about how his brothers were failing their responsibilities.

As a result, they hated Joseph and conspired to kill him. After some debate, they sold him into slavery instead of killing him. The caravan of slave traders took him to Egypt and sold him to the house of a man named Potiphar. Can we even imagine what it would be like to be a slave?

Slavery was an awful, terrible evil, and thankfully it has mostly been abolished in our modern day. A slave has absolutely no choice over his destiny, his direction or his decisions. Some masters were kinder and more tolerant than others, and some gave their slaves a degree of autonomy, but they were still owned. They couldn't quit or change jobs if they didn't like what they were told to do. And Joseph was a slave because his own brothers sold him into slavery.

2. Joseph Was Bought

Can you imagine standing on an auction block and listening to people talk about how much you were worth as a purchase? "I don't know about that one. He looks a little weak and wimpy. I wouldn't get a good day's work out of him. Look at his posture. He's probably going to have back problems."

Joseph was bought twice, first by the Midianites for their slave caravan, and then by Potiphar. People in difficult and unfair circumstances sometimes get angry and bitter. Sometimes they become resigned and just give up. Years ago I counseled with a young lady who grew up out in the country. Most of her friends were boys, and they took her along with them out into the woods.

After she got older, they began to take advantage of her physically. She was really struggling with that pain from her past. She told me, "After a while, I got to where I just didn't care anymore." She had become so degraded in her own mind that she didn't think it mattered whether she retained any dignity or decency.

Joseph, despite all that had happened to him, refused to lose his belief in who he was and who God was. As a result of his attitude and performance, Potiphar recognized that Joseph was a good worker and diligent and promoted him to a position of responsibility within his household.

3. Joseph Was Blessed

The Perception. Genesis 39:3 says, "And his master saw that the LORD was with him, and that the LORD made all that he did to prosper in his hand." It was clear to Potiphar that there was something different about this Hebrew slave. He recognized that the God Joseph served was doing something in his life. He saw that things went well when Joseph was involved.

The Promotion. Genesis 39:4 says, "And Joseph found grace in his sight, and he served him: and he made him overseer over his house, and all that he had he put into his hand."

> *The Devil tries to use good things to tempt us to sin.*

Notice the extent of Joseph's control—everything that Potiphar had was placed under his responsibility. Potiphar had such complete confidence in Joseph that "he knew not ought he had, save the bread which he did eat" (Gen. 39:6). Not only did Potiphar place Joseph in charge, he didn't even check up on him.

The Prosperity. Genesis 39:5 says, "And it came to pass from the time that he had made him overseer in his house, and over all that he had, that the LORD blessed the Egyptian's house for Joseph's sake; and the blessing of the LORD was upon all that he had in the house, and in the field." Everything Potiphar had did better because Joseph was there.

Over the years I've seen some people who were faithful to God when things were tough. As they struggled and worked and prayed, He responded and blessed them. But then when things started to go well, they turned away from Him. All of a sudden church wasn't so important anymore. Tithing gave way to saving for the beach house. They started to think things were going good because they were so special. That is a dangerous mindset to have.

The Seduction Attempted

Joseph was a young man (probably around eighteen years old) who, humanly speaking, had a reason to be bitter. He could have felt he had been abandoned by God. He was in a place where no one spoke his language or knew who he was. He had just received a promotion to a position of power and influence. It was in this setting that Joseph faced temptation.

1. The Appeal

Genesis 39:7 says, "And it came to pass after these things, that his master's wife cast her eyes upon Joseph; and she said, Lie with me." The Bible doesn't tell us the details, but from what history tells us, this was not unusual behavior. It was not uncommon for an owner to take a slave and have an improper relationship with him. Egypt was an ungodly, immoral and promiscuous society.

There is no indication that Potiphar's wife expected to be refused. She didn't check to see if he was interested; she didn't flirt with him; she just flat-out propositioned him. It seems likely that she had indulged herself in that kind of immoral relationship before without any consequences.

The appeal was based on Joseph's looks. Genesis 39:6 says, "Joseph was a goodly person, and well favoured." That's not two ways to say the same thing. Being "a goodly person" means he had a handsome face. He had what they call movie-star good looks. I saw a statue in a museum in Egypt that supposedly dates back to the time of Joseph. If that was he, he was indeed a good-looking guy. Calling Joseph "well favoured" means that he had a good physique. He was built and well-proportioned.

If we had a choice between having a good-looking child and an ugly child, most of us would rather have the good-looking child. I remember when we knew that Karissa was about to be born and we would be adopting her. Of course we didn't know what she would look like. I hadn't thought about it a lot before that, but I started watching babies.

All of a sudden it seemed like I was seeing ugly babies everywhere! I asked Krissy, "What if the baby is a girl and she turns out to be ugly?" My wife replied, "I was just thinking the same thing. If she is, we'll just put her in a pretty bonnet." The way you can tell Karissa wasn't ugly is that she's not in a bonnet in her baby pictures!

We would have loved her no matter what she looked like. But most people would choose to be better looking, and that's not a bad thing. Yet the Devil tries to use good things to tempt us to do bad things in our lives. Talent can tempt you to laziness. A good personality can tempt you to take advantage of others. Intelligence can tempt you to be proud. Good looks can tempt you to have improper relationships.

The appeal was based on Potiphar's wife's lust. It is reasonable to assume that Joseph was somewhat flattered by her proposition. I knew a man who is now in Heaven. He was staying in a motel at a conference with some other men from his church. Some lady came by and knocked on the door of his room. When she saw that there were other men in there with him, she went away somewhat embarrassed. He looked at the men (one of them told me the story) and said, "Well, fellows, it's nice to know that you still have it!"

That's not a very wise response. But it is in keeping with human nature. If we find out that someone thinks we are attractive, we're tempted to feel a little bit flattered. Mrs. Potiphar liked the way Joseph looked, so she invited him to join her in an evil relationship. Just because someone encourages you to do wrong doesn't mean you have to do it.

I told our girls when they got old enough to date (thirty-five sounds about right, doesn't it?), "Just because he wants a kiss doesn't mean he gets one!" Taking a girl out on a date doesn't give a guy any right to do wrong. No matter who encourages you to sin and how much pressure they put on you, you can still do right.

2. The Answer

It was immediate. Joseph did not take time to think it over. He didn't say she could ask again later. He didn't tell her it might not be a great idea. He simply said, "No." It is important to respond immediately when you are tempted. The longer you take to make a decision, the more likely you are to make a wrong decision.

> *The longer that you wait to respond when you are tempted, the more likely you are to fall to it.*

And Joseph didn't leave any room for doubt. "He refused," the Bible says. Franklin Jones said, "What makes resisting temptation difficult for many people is that they don't want to discourage it completely." Anytime you do not respond promptly when the Holy Spirit leads you, you place yourself at risk.

Years ago my father and I were in a bowling alley. We were talking about someone in the ministry who was going through some real struggles. I told him about the situation, and he said, "So he's really having financial trouble." I said he was, and Dad immediately reached into his wallet and pulled out a $50 bill and said, "Give this to them."

At the time he was between churches, and I knew that he didn't have a lot of money. I suggested he wait. He said, "No. I learned a long time ago that if I don't respond to generous impulses immediately, I'll talk myself out of doing what I ought to do." Do right, right away.

It was insightful. Joseph didn't just know the what; he knew the why. I encourage parents to spend time explaining to their kids why they have the rules they have for their family. It's good to have the rules, but it's not enough. Give them Bible reasons for the standards you hold. Ask them to explain the reasons to you.

Joseph said, "How then can I do this great wickedness, and sin against God?" (Gen. 39:9) He realized that yielding to the temptation might gratify his appetites, but it would displease God. We need a revival in this country of a proper view of sin. We have downplayed it and renamed it to make it less offensive to us. But God still hates sin. If we view it as He does, we will be much less likely to yield when we are tempted.

It was ineffective. Joseph gave the right response, but it didn't work. The Devil doesn't give up just because you say no once. It would be nice if things were that simple, but they're not. Knowing what is right and doing what is right when you are tempted are only the start.

The Devil will keep tempting you again and again, trying to see if he can catch you with your armor off and your guard down. He's patient. If he doesn't get you the first time, he'll come back. Even after Jesus refused his temptations, Satan only left for a little while. Luke 4:13 says, "And when the devil had ended all the temptation, he departed from him for a season."

The Sustained Attack

One of the reasons that Joseph's story is such a good example of how we should respond to temptation is that it so clearly illustrates this tactic of our enemy. He knows that over time, we become accustomed to sin, and it no longer repels us as it did when we first were exposed to it. This is true even if we continue to resist the temptation.

> **Vice is a monster of so frightful mien,**
> **As to be hated needs but to be seen;**
> **Yet seen too oft, familiar with her face,**
> **We first endure, then pity, then embrace.**

Alexander Pope

1. The Persistence

Genesis 39:10 says, "And it came to pass, as she spake to Joseph day by day, that he hearkened not unto her, to lie by her, or to be with her." Whatever else you can say about Mrs. Potiphar, she was persistent. You might think she would have given up when Joseph kept turning her down, but she was used to getting what she wanted.

Dealing with temptation is not a one-time issue; it's a daily issue. A pastor in the same state where I had a church had a female member with somewhat of a bad reputation. He tried to be very careful in guarding himself, because he suspected that she was pursuing him. One day when his wife was out of town, she came by his house, and you know the rest of the story.

> *Dealing with temptation is a daily issue.*

He said this, "For sixteen years I was squeaky clean. I messed up one time. Now I've ruined my ministry." And he had. The Devil tried and failed repeatedly to get that pastor to sin. He kept trying until he succeeded. There will never be a single day in your life when you are so strong that you are not in danger.

In fact, when you think you are strong, you are at even greater risk. Paul wrote,

> *"Now all these things happened unto them for ensamples: and they are written for our admonition, upon whom the ends of the world are come. Wherefore let him that thinketh he standeth take heed lest he fall."*—I Cor. 10:11, 12.

2. The Precaution

Genesis 39:11 says, "And it came to pass about this time, that Joseph went into the house to do his business; and there was none of the men of the house there within." He not only said no, he took steps not to be around her. If you linger in a place of temptation, you are setting yourself up for failure.

Years ago, we had someone on staff at our church in a part-time position. There was never any one thing that I could put my finger on, but I was a little uncomfortable about her. I talked to my wife, and she said, "I don't think she means anything wrong, but she could be led astray. Be careful."

In order to have victory over a particular temptation, you might have to completely sever a tie.

So I told my secretary, "Don't ever leave me alone here at the office with her. If I need to leave early and work at home, I will. But I want you to be sure you're here when she's here." Then I said, "Every time she comes into my office, interrupt us. Don't call or knock, just walk in. If you don't have any other excuse, write on a piece of paper, 'This is the piece of paper you told me to put on your desk!'"

One time this lady was having trouble with her feet. She

asked me to anoint her with oil and pray for her. I did, and when I finished praying, she kept standing there. So I said, "That's all," and walked her out of the office. Later I found out that she had been involved with several other people. I am so grateful that I was cautious around her.

Joseph made arrangements so that he would not be exposed to the temptation Mrs. Potiphar was offering him. If you know a program on television is bad, why keep watching it? If you know a radio station plays the wrong kind of music, change the button on the radio. Take precautions to help you do right.

3. The Prudence

The Bible says that Joseph "left his garment in her hand, and fled, and got him out" (Gen. 39:12). When his plans to avoid Mrs. Potiphar failed and she propositioned him again, he ran away. He didn't linger in her presence any longer. There comes a time when you just have to sever completely a tie that is drawing you to temptation.

Jesus said, "And if thy right eye offend thee, pluck it out, and cast it from thee" (Matt. 5:29). He was using a very strong hyperbolic argument to emphasize the importance of avoiding sin. He didn't say a person being tempted should wear sunglasses; He said he should pull his eye out!

Proverbs 22:3 says, "A prudent man foreseeth the evil, and hideth himself: but the simple pass on, and are punished." Try to stay away from any temptation which you can foresee. Then when you are tempted, flee. That is the advice Paul gave to Timothy, and it is vitally important for each of us (I Tim. 6:11; II Tim. 2:22).

The Secret Analyzed

We know from the Bible account that Joseph did not fall to the temptation that was brought against him. He paid a price for doing right, as Potiphar's wife then lied about him and had him put in prison. But God used even that to elevate Joseph to the position He planned for him to fill. So how did Joseph triumph over his temptation?

1. Joseph Remembered His Privilege

Joseph said, "Behold, my master wotteth not what is with me in the house, and he hath committed all that he hath to my hand" (Gen. 39:8). Potiphar had placed enormous trust and responsibility in Joseph. He had been given a privilege that was accorded to very few slaves.

It is a privilege to be a child of God. It is a privilege to be a servant of God. Never take the promise of I John 1:9 as an excuse to do whatever you want. Don't abuse your privileges. It is a wonderful truth that once we are saved, we are saved forever. There is nothing you can do that will cause you to lose your salvation. Yet that is not a license to sin.

Someone once told Charles Spurgeon, "If I believed what you believe about eternal security, I'd sin all I wanted!" Spurgeon replied, "I sin much more than I want." God has saved you and placed you into His family. Live up to that great privilege you have been given by grace.

2. Joseph Regarded His Position

Joseph said, "There is none greater in this house than I" (Gen. 39:9). He had been given a position of responsibility and prominence. There were things he could not do because of the job that he held.

I had a police officer once tell me about another officer who went to the gas pump at the station that was meant for filling up the squad cars. He pumped $13.00 worth of gas into his personal car and didn't pay for it. What he didn't know was that the transaction was caught on videotape. He lost his job and his pension and his years of service and his testimony for $13.00.

He should have said, "I'm a policeman. I can't steal. I'm in charge of keeping others from stealing. They put up warnings to people on gas pumps that if they drive off without paying, someone like me will arrest them. I have to do what is right because of my position." He did not focus on his position as a reason for right behavior, and, as a result, he lost that position.

3. Joseph Recognized the Principle

Joseph said, "Neither hath he kept back any thing from me but thee, because thou art his wife" (Gen. 39:9). That woman didn't belong to Joseph; she belonged to her husband, Potiphar. Joseph realized that taking her for his own, even if she wanted him to do so, would violate the principle of ownership.

Hugh Downs was for many years a newscaster for ABC. He was being interviewed once after he started working with Barbara Walters on 20/20. The interviewer asked, "Was there ever a time when you were attracted to her?" He said, "Well, I guess you could say I was aware she was an attractive woman."

The interviewer said, "What did you do about it?" Downs said, "Do? I didn't do anything. I was married!" That ought to be our attitude toward things that are off-limits. We should never even consider violating the principles of God's Word. It ought to be literally unthinkable to us.

The Devil tries to make sin look exciting and intriguing. I remember a trip I took some years ago to preach in New York. I flew out there a little early and wanted to spend some time sightseeing. I had the pastor I was speaking for give me some directions so I could find my way back, and went downtown. I've always liked big cities. I had a good time and witnessed to some people.

I saw a couple of guys in really scruffy clothes sitting on the sidewalk. They had a little cardboard setup with three cards on it. They would move the cards around, and you were supposed to guess which card was the red one. After watching them for a little while, I realized that the red card had a mark on it. I had taken thirty dollars with me, and I thought, *I could double my money by playing their game.*

I had one of those conversations with myself. *It's not right to gamble. But it's not gambling—I know which card the red one is!* I really thought about it (briefly), but I knew it was wrong and walked away. I went into a drugstore and talked to the man at the counter. "You could make a lot of money at that game," I said. He just smiled. "You'd win once," he said. "And then you'd lose everything you had." He explained to me that they have another marked card that looks like the red one, but is black. They use it after they get you into the game.

The reason I didn't gamble wasn't because I was afraid to lose. In fact, I was wrongly convinced that I would win. The reason I didn't gamble is that I recognized the principle and wasn't willing to violate it, even for something that looked like a sure thing.

4. Joseph Recognized the Problem

Joseph said, "How then can I do this great wickedness, and sin against God?" (Gen. 39:9). If you just look at things between you and other people, you can come up with all kinds of rationalizations for doing wrong. But if you look at things as being between you and God, that's pretty hard to do.

The bottom line for Joseph was that he did not want to sin against God. Other considerations influenced Joseph, but this is the one that overrode all others. Every sin is ultimately an act of defiance against God.

David said, "Against thee, thee only, have I sinned, and done this evil in thy sight: that thou mightest be justified when thou speakest, and be clear when thou judgest" (Ps. 51:4). David's sin affected a lot of other people. But he realized that the real issue was that he had sinned against God.

God loves you, and He sent His Son to die on the cross to pay for your sins. He saved you and sent His Holy Spirit to live within you and to give you guidance and comfort. He is the one that you need to be most concerned about when you are choosing whether or not to yield to temptation.

5. Review the Punishment

This principle isn't found directly in the story of Joseph, but I think it's also an important thing to remember when you are tempted. Think about what has happened to people who did the same thing you're thinking about doing. Think about where they ended up. Think about the wages of sin, not just the enticements of sin. What does the Bible say happens to people who do what you are thinking about doing?

Years ago there was a man who was teaching at a Bible college. People came to me and started telling me what a wonderful teacher he was. I listened to some tapes, and he was great. He had a way of explaining and expounding the Word of God that was really unique.

One day he called me and told me he was going to start a church. I told him that we would support him. Our church gave him money to help him get off the ground.

Later another pastor friend of mine was in the process of hiring a teacher for his school. He hired a young lady who had been working for that Bible teacher. He noticed that she seemed unusually nervous around him. He asked her if something had happened.

She began to cry, and the story emerged. This great and gifted Bible teacher had done a study with her on the subject of concubines. He had tried to twist the Scriptures to prove to her that it was all right for her to have an immoral relationship with him. She refused and left.

We quit supporting him! He eventually left where he was and took another church. He got in trouble there and began calling preachers around the country. He told a story that the city wanted the church property and to get it they had started a campaign of lies against him. He didn't call me, but he did call some preachers I knew. When I heard the story, it didn't ring true with me.

I told those men, "You need to face the possibility that he might not be telling the truth." Some of them decided to help him, and some of them didn't. Today that man sits in a jail cell where he is serving a life sentence for some awful and unspeakable acts. I wouldn't even begin to describe to you the things he has been convicted of doing.

I spent the summer of 1971 working on the staff of a church in Michigan. There was a sweet old man in that church who played the piano for them. He has long since been in Heaven. He made the trip along with some other people from that church to come to my wedding when Krissy and I got married.

At the wedding, my in-laws recognized him. He had previously lived in their city, where he worked as an accountant. He had stolen money from the company for which he worked. That man gave away all of the money that he stole to poor people! But the ends don't justify the means. He lost his job and moved away in disgrace. Years later the results of his sin still followed him.

If you stop and consider the consequences of sin, it will help keep you from doing wrong. Temptations are a certainty in this life, but they do not have to defeat you. First

Corinthians 10:13 says, "There hath no temptation taken you but such as is common to man: but God is faithful, who will not suffer you to be tempted above that ye are able; but will with the temptation also make a way to escape, that ye may be able to bear it." You can live right, even under the pressure of the Devil.

3

When You Have a Baby

"Except the LORD build the house, they labour in vain that build it: except the LORD keep the city, the watchman waketh but in vain.

"It is vain for you to rise up early, to sit up late, to eat the bread of sorrows: for so he giveth his beloved sleep.

"Lo, children are an heritage of the LORD: and the fruit of the womb is his reward.

"As arrows are in the hand of a mighty man; so are children of the youth.

"Happy is the man that hath his quiver full of them: they shall not be ashamed, but they shall speak with the enemies in the gate."—Ps. 127:1–5.

It's amazing what happens to a household when a little baby comes to live there. That little, amazing, incredible, miraculous, bundle of flesh you gaze at with wonder and awe changes everything in your life. The first cry is so special. But then after a while, you wish you would never hear that sound again.

When Karissa was first born and came to live at our house, one of my friends gave me some advice. He said,

"The best way in the world to ruin your life is going without any sleep. So here's what you do. Put the baby on one end of the house, and you sleep at the other end of the house—and close as many doors between you and that baby as you can!"

People change when babies come. All of a sudden, people who've been faithful in church can't get there. Now two grown adults have to stay home all day because one ten-pound baby has the sniffles. Some people change so that life revolves entirely around the baby. Serious intellectual adults become driveling idiots when a baby comes.

Now babies are a blessing. Babies are good; the Bible says they're the heritage of the Lord. And it's a happy man whose quiver is full of children. But sometimes babies are an excuse for people to backslide too. Sometimes babies cause division and difficulty between the husband and wife. Having children is a crisis stage of life. Crisis is not always a bad thing. The Chinese symbol for the word crisis is made up from two other symbols—the symbols for danger and opportunity. Children represent both a danger and a tremendous opportunity.

The Dangers

Why do people sometimes backslide when they have babies? Why do husbands and wives find their relationship becoming strained? Why do children represent a danger?

1. Wrong Purposes

Sometimes people want children for the wrong reasons. And if you want children for the wrong reasons, it is likely that they will be a source of trouble and contention. Here are some common wrong reasons that people desire children.

To be like others. Couples sometimes feel like everybody

else has a baby except them. That is natural, and it's understandable, but that is not a good reason to have a child. To invest hundreds of thousands of dollars and eighteen or twenty years of your life just so you can be like everybody else is not why God gives children to their parents.

To possess the child. I think you should love your baby and show the baby off. I think you should hold the baby out and say to everybody, "Isn't she beautiful?" When I go into hospitals right after a baby is born, invariably the mother looks at me and says, "Pastor, isn't he beautiful?" I'm a man of God, and I don't want to lie. I say "Wow, you must really be excited!" I'm glad that you love your child and enjoy having the child, but that's not a right reason to want children in your life.

To be loved. A young married man once said to me that he and his wife wanted to have a baby. They were exploring different options, he said, because they wanted to experience the kind of love that you can get only from a little child. Now what happens if you have a child because you want that kind of love, and one day you don't get that love anymore? I understand there is a wonderful, innocent, unselfish love that comes from little children. It's tremendously enjoyable, and I think it's of the Lord. But that's not a right motive to have a child.

To impress others. I know some people who have trained their children and show them off like they'd show off a dog. Now I think you ought to train your children. But you need to discipline them for the right reasons. Don't spank your kids because you're embarrassed; spank them because you're trying to teach them to do right. Some people want to use their children to demonstrate that they are the perfect parents.

To fill a void in their life. Whether you are childless or your quiver is full, whether you're fifty-five and single or you have been married for thirty years, you are, no matter what your circumstance, complete in Christ. In the Lord Jesus you have everything that you need. Some of the greatest Christians in the world have never married nor had children. You don't have to have children to be complete. Children are wonderful, and they fill a place in our lives that nothing else can. But that is not a right reason to have children.

2. Wrong priorities

Another thing that happens when people have children is that they sometimes adopt wrong priorities in their lives. Children are precious and vital, and rearing them properly requires an enormous investment of time and energy. But some parents place their children too high on the scale of priorities in life. Here are some of the attitudes I've encountered that indicate misplaced priorities.

> *Children are given to you for you to rear and then give back to God for His service.*

I am going to spend every moment possible with this child. I believe children are and should be a high priority in life. But some people take that to extremes. They say, "No bus route, no soul winning, no Sunday night church, no Wednesday night church. That's cutting into our family time." I'm all for family time. But there is nothing more important that you can teach your children than to love God. And it's pretty hard to tell them to love God first when you put everything else ahead of Him. Children will see your real priorities (not just what you say) and make value judgments accordingly. Rearing children properly requires a huge time investment, but do not take that time away from God and His work.

I am going to build my life around this child. Can I tell you something? Your children are not going to live in your house

42

forever. And if you build your entire life around them, you are going to face a huge letdown when they are gone. I think you ought to have other interests. I think you ought to be involved at your church with ministries that you can do with your children and ministries you can do when your children are gone. When our girls were very small, I began preparing my heart for the day when they would leave.

I am never going to let this child out of my sight. I understand the impulse to protect your child from an evil world. That is one of the most important jobs of parents. But it is physically impossible to guard your children twenty-four hours per day. We have known people who never invited others to their house, never got involved in the ministries of the church and never did anything else so that they could be with their children. It is unhealthy for both parents and children to have that kind of focus.

I am going to shield my child from anything negative. Now please understand this—I do not agree with the philosophy that says you should expose your children to wrong ideas so they learn how to handle them. I warn the people in our church about letting children watch garbage on television and letting them have the wrong friends. That is not what I'm talking about here. I know a man who was once a helpful and encouraging preacher. Now he doesn't believe anybody should teach children except their parents. He doesn't believe in Sunday school. He really doesn't believe in the church; instead he promotes home church. That is promoting an unhealthy level of isolation. We are to be *in* the world, but not *of* it.

My dad took over the Detroit City Rescue Mission when I was in the first grade. For the next ten years, my Dad ran that rescue mission. I would sometimes get on a bus and ride from my house in the northwest section of Detroit to downtown Detroit and walk to the rescue mission. We had camps in the summer and kids from the inner city of Detroit, and I'd hang around those guys that were at the mission in the program. I learned so many things from that experience that God used to equip me for ministry. He also used that experience to protect me from some things.

I'm fifty-four years old, and I've yet to have my first drink of alcohol. There are plenty of things I've done wrong and plenty of things I wish I hadn't done, and there are plenty of things that could still tempt me today, but booze is not one of them. Do you know why? Because in a controlled environment I saw that what the Devil delivered was not what he promised. I think one of the best things you can do for your children is to let them work on a church bus route. I wanted my children to be aware that there are people that have burdens and needs and we need to win them to Christ and see them delivered from that.

Some parents are so committed to shielding their child from anything negative that they don't want them to serve God. Years ago a sweet young lady from a family in our church went home and said, "Mom and Dad, I made a really wonderful decision today in chapel. I've surrendered my life, and I'm going to be a missionary." By the way, if your kids ever say that, praise God. They may be in only the third grade, and their plans may change, but don't ever tell them not to obey God. Her parents told her they weren't going to let her go to some dangerous place where they couldn't protect her and she'd be exposed to all those negative things. So she didn't go. Eventually she married a guy of whom her parents approved. But after they had been married just a few months, he left her pregnant to raise their child alone. Your children are not yours to keep; they are not just for you to shelter from everything you think is bad. They are for you to rear to serve God.

It's God's job to decide where your children should be.

You ought to protect them, you ought to be careful, but you need to give your children to God to let them be used wherever He wants them to be. Your kids are safer in the most dangerous jungle in the will of God than they are in the safest American city outside the will of God. It's not your job to put them in the safest environment you can imagine; it's your job to put them inside the will of God. What's coming into your home on the television every day can do a whole lot more harm to your child than seeing what happens on a bus route ever will.

3. Wrong Product

We (not just the lost world but even within the church) are rearing a generation of pampered, protected, coddled, self-centered brats who think the world revolves around them. We don't spank them when they disobey as three-year olds, and then we wonder why they rebel and burn down buildings as eighteen-year olds. The wrong methods will never produce the right result. Many people like the end product of godly parenting; they just aren't willing to put forth the effort it requires.

The Declaration

Children are a heritage. In 1897, my great-great-grandfather gave my great-grandfather an Elgin pocket watch. He said it was solid gold (it's actually gold-filled), and it came with a twenty-year guarantee. It has an inscription that says, "February 18, 1897, given to Albert Bach by his parents." When I wear a suit with a vest, I often wear that watch. It is now more than 100 years old. My great-great-grandfather gave it to my great-grandfather, who gave it to my grandfather. When my grandmother died, my mother got the watch, and she gave it to me. I'm not going to keep it; I'm going to pass it on. I will probably give it to my first grandson.

45

Children are not just for you; they are for you to pass on to the next generation. If you have a daughter, you are rearing your future son-in-law's wife. If you have a son, you are rearing your future daughter-in law's husband. If you have children, you are rearing your grandchildren's parents! It's not about you; it's about the next generation. When I first came to the First Baptist Church of Bridgeport, I thought that in thirty years I would still be the pastor. I don't think that now. I'd be eighty-four! What I'm doing now is working to prepare the people the next pastor will lead after I am gone. That is the purpose of every parent—to prepare our children for the future.

1. The Posterity

A heritage is something given to a person to be passed on from generation to generation. He should not take credit for it, because it has been given to him. I repeat so you will get this: children are not for you to keep. They are for you to rear to give back to God, equipped for His service. The Bible describes children as arrows (Ps. 127:4). Arrows were a unique weapon in Bible days. They extended the ability of a soldier far beyond his reach. Most weapons, such as swords and spears, are limited in their impact on the enemy to the length of the arm of the soldier. But arrows greatly increased the ability of a soldier to strike. Your children extend your life and ministry far beyond what you will be able to do in your own lifetime.

Rear your children so that they are more valuable to God than you are.

I recently read about the violin that Joshua Bell plays. Bell is considered to be one of the top violinists in the world. He plays a Stradivarius made by the master violin-maker in 1713. He paid $3.5 million for this violin because of the incredible sound it produces. Nearly three hundred years of use have not diminished the value of the violin—in fact they have increased it. You can train your children in such a way that they are more valuable to God than you were. And you can train them in such a way that your grandchildren and great-grandchildren will still walk in His paths.

2. The Person

Children are given to us as a trust, and it is only a temporary trust. Again, my children are not mine to keep; they are mine for just a little while until they grow up. We have a few people in our church who have asked me to be the trustee for their wills. They have asked me to accept the responsibility for making sure things are done right if something happens to them. Some have even asked me if I would be responsible for rearing their children if they died.

That's exactly what God is asking you to do. He has given you children to train for Him. Many years ago, Dr. John R. Rice preached the funeral for a little girl who died when she was just eight years old. One of the things he told the grieving parents was that all of their children, the three who were living and the one now in Heaven, belonged to God. Since He has trusted them to us, we have an awesome responsibility to teach them to love Him. Children are not a reason to cut back on serving God; they are a reason to serve Him more faithfully.

3. The Propensity

We've already looked at Psalm 127:4 where children are compared to arrows. Have you ever shot a bow? I have. And I can tell you that the arrow does not always go where I want it to go—but it does always go where I aim it! I've missed the target a few times, but the fault is not in the arrow. The Bible is telling us that our children are going to head in the direction we point them.

A lot of parents don't approve of the way their children live as adults. The time to influence those choices is when they are small. My parents were strict. I tell people my mother spanked me for practice, she spanked me for recreation, and she spanked me (on the few times) when I did wrong. Someone told my father once he was going to warp me if he kept spanking me, and he said, "That's exactly what I'm trying to do! I'm trying to change his direction."

Have you ever housebroken a dog? Every time I've done it, it involved a lot of spanking. What happens after you spank your dog? Invariably mine would come back crouching and rub against my ankles and look at me to see if I was still mad. The dog wanted to make sure everything was fine again. Now what would happen if I spanked your dog? It would probably bite me. That's because I don't have any relationship with your dog. Discipline without a loving relationship is very ineffective. So here's the declaration: Your children belong to God, He's the one who gives them to you in trust, you have a responsibility to train them for Him, and they're going to tend to go where you point them.

The Duty

1. The Privilege

There are many people that would like to have babies who have been unable to have them. For years my wife and I prayed for children. After ten years of marriage, we were able to adopt a daughter. Five years later, our second daughter was born. It grieves me when I hear people say things like, "Oh, these children! I don't know what I'm going to do with them. I can't wait for school to start back." Children are precious. I'd much rather hear someone say, "Oh, no. School is about to start. It's back to homework and practices and all those things that fill up the schedule so I don't get to spend time with my child." I like that attitude. It shows a parent who appreciates the privilege of rearing children for God.

2. The Priority

When the angel came to Samson's parents to tell them they were going to have a son, they did not say, "Cool. We're going to have a baby." The very first thing they wanted to know was, "How do we rear him?" (Judges 13:10–12). When you have a child in your home, the first thing you ought to do is find out what

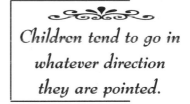

Children tend to go in whatever direction they are pointed.

the Bible says you ought to do as a parent. Ask, "What are my responsibilities and requirements as a child of God to rear another child of God who's been placed in my home?"

3. The Plan

Train them up. Proverbs 22:6 says, "Train up a child in the way he should go: and when he is old, he will not depart from it." The Hebrew word translated "train" is the word for sharpening something like an axe or a sword. It implies a careful and repeated process of honing to reach the desired result. Biblical child training is not a casual or occasional process. It requires repetition, consistency and love.

Turn them loose. When I counsel young people preparing to get married, I say, "After you get married, you still need to honor your parents. You need to listen to their advice, and you should seek their counsel. But you need to be sure you don't let them run your life." God's plan, all the way back to the first wedding between Adam and Eve, is for the new couple to leave their parents. Don't try to hang on to your children after they are grown and gone. I'm not saying you shouldn't be close to your children after they get married; in fact, I think it's wonderful. But you are not in charge of their lives anymore, and you need to remember that as you interact with them.

The Directions

1. Children Should Be an Addition to Your Schedule, Not an Alteration

Certainly it is a major change when children come into the home. There are few more dramatic transitions in life. But if you were reading the Bible every day before, make sure you read the Bible every day afterwards. If you were faithful to church, don't stop going. If you were involved in a ministry, keep on. Add your children to your life rather than allowing them to dominate it.

2. Children Should Have Parents Who Are Godly Examples

When Karissa was very young, I was looking for advice from a man who'd done a good job of rearing his children. One of the things he said was, "I run scared all the time." He was afraid that he would do something that would lead his children away from God. I wanted to be sure that my daughters knew their father lived what he preached.

> *Biblical child training requires repetition, consistency and love.*

3. Children Should Be Given Constant Spiritual Instruction

The Bible pattern is to teach your children, "when thou sittest in thine house, and when thou walkest by the way, and when thou liest down, and when thou risest up" (Deut.

6:7). Always be teaching your children the truths of the Word of God. Take advantage of things that happen to show them from the Bible what God says about what they have seen and heard.

4. Children Should Be Secondary to Their Parents' Relationship to God and to Each Other

Leave your children home some night and go out and have a nice meal with your husband or wife. That relationship is going to last long after your children leave home, and you need to be investing in it on a daily basis. Children are a tremendous distraction from other things. If you are going to maintain a good relationship with God and with your spouse, it will have to be done on purpose.

5. Parents Should Serve God With Their Children

Where do people get the idea that they have to choose between serving God and family time? I think you ought to have fun times and relaxing times and do fun things together, but I think that your children should also be involved in the work of God with you. That can also be family time. I would suggest that it's better family time than sitting at home watching a Disney video or some dumb TV show.

> *The goal in parenting is to prepare your children so that when they are on their own, they will make the right choices.*

I grew up in the work of God. My dad ran the Detroit Rescue Mission, and every Sunday afternoon we'd go down and eat lunch there, eating the same food the men at the mission ate. Then we'd have a service. Sometimes I'd lead the singing, and sometimes I'd play my trumpet. It is not a strange thing to me to serve God; it's not a strange thing to my children to serve

God. By the way, they don't wonder if we're going to go to church while we're on vacation, and neither should yours. I am not at all saying that you shouldn't take a vacation, but don't take a vacation from God.

6. Children Should See the Privilege of Obedience to God and the Price of Disobedience to God

From the time that our daughters were in grade school, I took them with me when I went out soul winning. I wanted them to learn that witnessing and serving God are a privilege we have as His children. It is not enough for parents to teach children to obey them. First and foremost, obedience is to God. If the children have the right attitude toward Him, the other things will take care of themselves.

7. Children Should Learn to Give, to Serve and to Gain Spiritual Insight for Themselves

We live in a very selfish society. Children need to learn that not everything in life is about them. They need to give of themselves. They need to serve others. I was preaching at a church one time, and there was a little boy about nine or ten years old whose job was to put the water on the pulpit for the speaker. He came up to me and said, "Dr. Ouellette, how do you like your water? Do you like it with ice or without ice?" Now somebody taught that boy that it is a big deal to do something for God and for the servants of God. That is a great lesson for your children. Remember that the ultimate goal of parenting is to prepare your children so that when they are on their own, they will make the right choices.

4

When Your Children Become Teenagers

One of the most difficult times of life in our society is when children become teenagers. The statistics on teenagers are painfully grim. Even among Christians, teens are more likely to commit suicide, start using drugs or alcohol and struggle with depression than are most other age groups. Over the years I have seen children who seemed to be doing well in grade school become rebellious and troublesome when they become teens.

Many times parents who felt like they had it together when their kids were younger suddenly feel like the worst failures in the world when they begin to deal with the issues of the teen years. There are definite problems and issues that teens have—but there are also things that parents can do that will help alleviate them.

The Disclaimer

1. The Term and Concept of *Teenager* Are Not in the Bible

The only two categories of people that we find in

Scripture are children and adults. There are no references in God's Word to tweenagers or teenagers. Those are societal terms that we use to identify and categorize people by their age. Now by saying that, I do not mean that it is unscriptural or wrong to call someone a teenager. But we should understand that it is not a Bible concept.

Nor was it even a societal concept until very recently. Author and researcher Robert Epstein, who wrote the book *The Case Against Adolescence: Rediscovering the Adult in Every Teen,* said this: "Unfortunately, the dramatic changes set in motion by the turmoil of America's industrial revolution also obliterated from modern consciousness the true abilities of young people, leaving adults with the faulty belief that teenagers were inherently irresponsible and incompetent. What's more, the rate at which restrictions were placed on young people began to accelerate after the 1930s and increased dramatically after the social turmoil of the 1960s. Surveys I've conducted suggest that teenagers today are subject to *ten times* as many restrictions as are mainstream adults, *twice* as many restrictions as are active-duty U.S. Marines, and even *twice* as many restrictions as are incarcerated felons."

2. Society Is Not the Same as Scripture

Since the concept of teenagers is not from the Bible but from society, we need to be on guard against adopting society's wrong philosophies and approaches. Doing something just because society says to do it isn't right. From time to time I hear people say things like: "Well, I just think that when they become teenagers, they should make their own decisions," or, "Well, you know once they're teenagers, you just can't tell them what to do all the time," or, "We don't want to restrict them too much, because if we did they'd probably just get mad and run away." Those are wrong philosophies. Just because Dr. Laura and Dr. Phil or Oprah say something doesn't mean that it is so.

The Difficulties

1. The Difficulties With Teenagers

You have this cute little elementary school kid living in your house. You hug him and kiss him every night when you put him to bed. Then one morning you wake up to discover that some alien from outer space has inhabited his body. He doesn't want to kiss you any more; he doesn't want to hug you anymore.

They don't want to tell you everything that happened at school. They don't want to play games with the family. They don't like to bounce on your knee anymore. They don't want to wrestle on the floor anymore. You ask, "What happened? Where did my loving child go?" Why does this change occur? Here are some of the things that happen.

They are becoming more independent. Part of the process of growing up is that they don't want your help as much as they did before. When a girl is little, she wants her mother to fix her hair. When she's in the sixth grade, she is no more qualified to fix her hair than she was in the third grade, but she wants to do it herself.

> *Be careful not to interpret the normal processes of growing up as rejection.*

I remember when my dad came in and said, "Son, you're growing up, and you're getting some whiskers. Would you like me to show you how to shave?" I told him, "No. I already know how." How did I know how to shave? I had watched a Gillette commercial on television. I figured that since I was thirteen years old, I wouldn't need any help shaving. And you know, 732 Band-Aids later, I finally figured it out. Teens are becoming more independent. Remember that this is not a bad thing. God's plan is not for them to live with you forever! You are preparing them to start a family of their own.

They are less dependent on their parents' help and opinions. If you tell your seven- or eight-year old, "I don't think that sweater looks good with that skirt or those slacks," they're likely to go get another one. If you tell your seventeen-year old that, they look at you like you're an idiot. You'll never convince me that orange and purple and yellow go together! Teens are developing their own style and preferences.

They are more desirous of doing things their own way. I remember one time my mother gave our daughter Karissa a watch. That was a very nice, expensive and generous gift. For some reason, Karissa put it on her right hand. And my mother said, "No, sweetie, that goes on your left hand." Karissa said, "I want to wear it on my right hand." They went back and forth for quite a while, because Karissa wanted to do it her own way. That is very common among teenagers.

They are becoming less communicative. Little kids want to tell you what happened during the day while they were gone. Teenagers don't mention anything unless there is blood involved, and sometimes not even then! They are drawing more into themselves and their age group. It is important not to take this normal process as a rejection. We'll talk more in a little bit about how parents should respond at this stage.

They are becoming less responsive. I have been a pastor for a long time. Over the years I've noticed how eager little children are to run up and give me a hug. They love their preacher, and I think that's a good thing. But teenagers—it's been a long time since a big, strapping teenage boy ran up to me in the hall and gave me a hug.

They still love, but their responses and the way they express themselves have changed.

They are becoming less affectionate. It really bothers a lot of parents because when their children were little they ran and hugged them and gave them all kinds of kisses. Now when they try to kiss their teens, the teens sigh like they are getting a public flogging and they have to stand there and take it. Parents need to work to keep expressing affection even when it is not being returned with enthusiasm.

They are insecure. By the way, this is the reason for most of the symptoms we discussed in the last two points. I've heard people say, "Young people are living in the best time of their life. Those were the golden years. What have they got to worry about?" Those people are nuts! I wouldn't want to be a teenager again for ANYTHING! Do you remember being a teen? You would go to pick up a glass of milk, but your arm had grown two inches since the last time you picked up a glass, and you ended up spilling the whole thing. You felt like your face was one large zit. Your parents should have bought stock in Clearasil. Teenagers are worried about fitting in because so many things are changing in their lives.

> *Keep expressing affection even when it is not returned with enthusiasm.*

They are more concerned with the opinions of their peers than that of their parents. When your children are little, you are their whole world. About all a baby knows is his mom and dad. They feed him, hug him, burp him and change him. He's aware that there are other people in the world, but he is absolutely dependant on his parents. He couldn't make it without them. But by the time that child becomes a teenager, you are only a part of his world. And I hate to tell you this, but you're not even the most important part.

When Karissa was in the first grade, she had Theresa Hintz for her teacher. One day Karissa came home and asked me a question. I told her the answer, and she said "No, Dad, that's not the answer. That's not what Miss Hintz said." I told her that Miss Hintz might be mistaken but that I had the right answer. She said, "NO, Dad, Miss Hintz said that wasn't the answer!" That day it dawned on me. Our first daughter was in the first grade. She was not going to believe everything I said all the time anymore. I was no longer the only authority in her life.

Teens are more concerned about their peers' opinions than that of their parents. Do you ever wonder why teenagers do such weird things? When I was a kid, if you had walked to school wearing some of the things that these kids have on and with your hair fixed some of the ways they have theirs fixed, you would have been laughed out of the town. We never did things like that. Never! We were too busy putting Brylcreem on our hair and pulling it back into a ducktail. We couldn't afford to spend all that time spiking our hair, because we were too busy getting our feet into blue jeans that were about three inches wide at the bottom. We would never have done the things these teenagers are doing today. Do you know why we did the things we did? One simple reason: that's what the other kids were doing. We copied what our peers were doing.

2. Difficulties With Parents

Some parents exercise excessive and unnecessary control. Because parents want to be a part of the child's life and make sure he turns out right, they sometimes micromanage every detail and minute part of his life. Discern the difference between that which is contrary to what you prefer and that which is wrong. I try really hard in making rules for the school to distinguish between what I think is stupid and what I think is sinful.

I do not think you should ever let your children do wrong so that they can "find themselves" or exercise their independence. But if it is not a matter of principle, allow them room to express their individual taste and style. They do not have to do everything according to your preferences in order to be good and godly children.

Some parents quit exercising appropriate control. Sometimes parents get tired of the battles. They've tried to hold the line, and they get tired of doing it. So they just give up and allow the children to do whatever they want. They take the easy way out by letting them make their own decisions, even if those decisions are wrong.

Never allow your children to do things that you know are wrong. Even if everybody is doing it, they do not have to be allowed to participate. You may sometimes feel that you are the only one who is making your children do right. That is probably not true, but even if it is, hold the line on what is right and wrong. Stick to your guns. Set and enforce rules for everyone who lives in your house.

Some parents quit talking and start preaching. I tell the people in our church, "What I do in the pulpit and what I do in the office counseling people are entirely different." The tone and demeanor you adopt will go a long way toward determining how your child responds to what you are saying.

Some parents seem to think they need to keep on saying something until the child agrees. The problem with that approach is there is an "OFF" switch in the mind of the teenager that is automatically set to trip about thirty seconds into a lecture. You are not reaching them by repeating a lecture over and over again. Make your point briefly and clearly.

Some parents demonstrate less affection. If your mailbox responds more to a hug than your teenager does, hug him anyway. Do not back off from telling and showing your love for him. Most people do not realize how they come across to others. Parents can convey a message to their children that they have stopped loving them by failing to continue to express their affection.

> *Love, unexpressed, dies.*

Mrs. John R. Rice used to say, "Love, unexpressed, dies." Now this is not to say that you should embarrass your fifteen-year-old son by kissing him in public. But continue to show your love both verbally and physically even after your children become teenagers. Find ways to let them know that you still care. Remember that, as we've already seen, they are very insecure. They need to be reassured that your love is unchanging.

Some parents forget the emotions of the teenage years. When I was in junior high school, they had what they called a "Slam Book." The students would take turns writing down what they thought of others. I remember the day that I read what was written on my page. They made fun of my clothes. My father was running the Detroit City Rescue Mission then, and all my clothes came from the mission. We didn't have money for anything else.

I hadn't paid a lot of attention to it until then; but at that moment, I would have done anything—good or bad, right or wrong—to be accepted by my peers. I grew out of that emotion. But it was very real. And when my children struggle with rejection, isolation or other problems, I need to take their emotions seriously, because they are very real to them. It may not be a big deal to me, but that is not the standard that needs to be applied.

The Directions

1. Nurture Them

Nurture tends to be thought of as cuddly and comforting. But the root of the word implies correction and instruction in the truth. Make sure they know what is right. When my girls were little, we acted out Bible stories. When we got done, I would ask them what lesson the story taught us.

Please do not make the mistake of thinking that because you put your children in a Christian school or made sure they were involved in the youth group or took them to Sunday school, you have done your job. All those things can be tools to help you, but they do not replace the training you must do. They are supplements, but they are not substitutes. You are always to be teaching your children, no matter where you are or what you are doing (Deut. 6:6–9).

Sometimes we make the mistake of trying to teach our children everything that is wrong before we teach them what is right. I have read that the Chinese banking families would let their very young children play with real money. They never showed them counterfeit money. By the time they were old enough to work at the bank, they were so familiar with the real money that they could instantly recognize counterfeit currency.

The best defense against error is not to study every variation of error that is in the world, but to study the truth. If you know the truth intimately and personally, the errors do not hold the same appeal. Remember how Jesus responded to Satan's temptation? He answered every challenge by quoting the Scriptures. He knew the truth.

2. Admonish Them

Admonition refers to calling attention to something. When they fail to use good manners, remind them. The only way admonition works is if you have taught them the right behavior first. Most parents are focused much more on admonition than on nurturing. We find the faults and call attention to them.

Admonition outside the context of nurturing is a recipe for resentment and rebellion. Years ago a well-known preacher said, "No child goes to the Devil if he believes that one person genuinely cares for him." I believe there is a lot of truth in that statement. Sadly, that preacher's own son grew up to be a wicked and immoral man. He was admonished, but not nurtured. God holds him responsible for his own sins, but the reality is that his father failed to teach him properly.

3. Do Not Provoke Them

Provoking a child to wrath refers to more than just disappointing him with a decision or enforcing a rule. It is talking about the result of continual nagging and the arbitrary assertion of authority. All of God's commands in the Bible are important, but I believe the negative commands (the "thou shalt not" commands) carry greater weight and importance. So not provoking our children is critical to maintaining a right relationship with them.

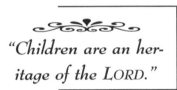

"Children are an heritage of the LORD."

Parents are supposed to be nice to their children. You are supposed to treat them with respect. Even when you are disciplining them or when they do not agree with your decision, they should never walk away feeling like they have been treated disrespectfully. They should not be able to honestly complain about your disposition and demeanor, even if they complain about your decision.

If you are trying to discipline while you are frustrated, you are much more likely to fall into the trap of saying the right thing in the wrong way. Your tone and word choice are probably at least as important as what you are trying to convey, if not more so. Do not provoke your children.

It is true that they should obey you "because I said so." They are responsible to obey. But if you are throwing the weight of your authority around in an arbitrary manner, you are provoking anger. There should be a reason for what you are doing. I do not believe you always have to explain first. We taught our daughters, "First you obey; then we explain." If you do not explain the reasons behind the rules, they will not learn and internalize what you are trying to teach them. Then when they get out on their own, those rules will quickly fall by the wayside.

4. Remember Your Stewardship

"Lo, children are an heritage of the LORD" (Ps. 127:3). They do not belong to you; they are just on loan from and for Him. A heritage is something passed on to the next generation. Remember this: you are rearing your grandchildren's parents. A good steward does not work to satisfy himself or to impress others, but to please God.

You need to be faithful and diligent in rearing your children. The work that you are doing is not just for you or even for them, but for God. I know many parents who wish they could go back now that their children are grown and undo some mistakes that they made. It is far better to do all that you can while your children are still young.

The Detailed Instructions

1. Remember They Are Gradually Becoming Independent

Part of your goal as your children become teenagers is to teach them to make right choices. The only way to do that is to teach them what is right and wise, and then turn them loose to make decisions on their own. You have to give them options so that they can learn how to choose between right and wrong.

Teach them that there are consequences when they make a wrong choice—and allow them to suffer those conse-

> *Teach your children, whatever the age, to make right choices.*

quences. Of course you should not allow them to be injured, but if you protect your children every time, they will not learn what they need to know to make wise decisions. Allow them to make choices, not between right and wrong, but between good and acceptable.

2. Treat Them With Respect and Dignity

I hardly ever raise my voice when I am dealing with teenagers. Speak to them like you would speak to an adult. Do not call them names or belittle them. Do not point out their faults in public. Do not do anything that is meant to embarrass them.

Remember that teenagers are very unsure of their place in the world and, therefore, very insecure. When you speak to them with respect, it makes it easier for them to show you the proper respect in return. In addition, it softens their heart to prepare them to listen to what you have to say rather than rejecting it out of anger at the way in which it is said.

3. Relate to Them

Remember how you felt as a teen. When I am dealing with a teenager, I try to remember what it felt like when I was facing a similar issue in my life. Emotions are very close to the surface and very real to teens, and you need to try to identify with those emotions as you talk to them.

Ask God to help you understand what they think. Pray for wisdom to discern what their real issue is. Frequently they will not tell you the real concern they have at first. So encourage them to keep talking until they arrive at the underlying problem. Put yourself in their position.

Tell them how you used to feel. So many teenagers think they are the only ones who have ever felt the way they do. Simply finding out that someone else has been through similar issues is a real comfort. Talking through your experiences also helps you empathize with their struggles and emotions.

Tell them what you suspect they might feel. Sometimes I will say to a teen, "Let me guess how you feel. You want to grow up and marry someone who loves you. You want to have a good life. But maybe you think it would be easier if the rules weren't quite as strict." Then I'll ask them if I'm right or wrong.

Ask them questions that lead to the truth you want them to see. People will not listen to you until they think you understand them. Whether you actually understand is irrelevant; what matters is that they think you do. By asking questions, you make them feel that you are taking the time to "get it," and then they will be prepared mentally to listen to what you say.

4. Demonstrate Love and Affection, Even If It Is Not Reciprocated

Do this appropriately, but faithfully. Parents stop showing affection when the child stops returning it. Then when the child wants to receive it again, the parent is out of the habit. Continue to say, "I love you," even if all you get is a grunt in return.

Things are changing very rapidly for teenagers. They need to know that there is a constant and unchanging love from their parents that they can count on. It may be several years before they acknowledge it, but if you continue to verbalize and show your love, it will be a huge help to them in staying on the right path.

5. Treat Minor Infractions Lightheartedly

That does not mean that you do not deal with them, but it does mean that you do not make a federal capital case out of a misdemeanor. There are times when your children need to see you grieve, and there may even be times when they need to see you angry, but this should be reserved for truly serious matters.

Many times parents overreact because they are embarrassed by what the child has done rather than responding with appropriate severity to the actual offense. Teenagers are acutely aware of this kind of hypocrisy, and they will not respect a parent who is upset over being embarrassed rather than over what was done wrong.

6. Have Established Principles and Penalties

Set the rules and punishments ahead of time so that the child knows the consequences of the choice. Simply enforce the appropriate penalty when the rule is broken. By doing this, you eliminate a lot of the drama and fighting that often accompanies punishment.

My father used to sit across from me and ask, "What did you do?" I would tell him. Then he would say, "And what did we say was going to happen if you did [or didn't do] that?" Again I would supply my own noose for the hanging. Then he would simply enforce whatever the punishment was. Because of the way he handled it, I didn't have anything to get upset over. I didn't like the process, but I knew it was fair.

7. Pray

If you have a problem with your child, set aside fifteen minutes a day when you do nothing but pray for him. That is a lot harder than it sounds. Praying specifically for one thing for fifteen minutes requires focus and discipline. Enter into spiritual warfare on behalf of your child.

Pray that God will turn his heart toward Him. Ephesians 6:12 says, "For we wrestle not against flesh and blood, but against principalities, against powers, against the rulers of the darkness of this world, against spiritual wickedness in high places." God will do amazing things if you are faithful to pray.

5

When Your Children Leave Home

"And he [Jesus] *said, A certain man had two sons:*

"And the younger of them said to his father, Father, give me the portion of goods that falleth to me. And he divided unto them his living.

"And not many days after the younger son gathered all together, and took his journey into a far country, and there wasted his substance with riotous living.

"And when he had spent all, there arose a mighty famine in that land; and he began to be in want.

"And he went and joined himself to a citizen of that country; and he sent him into his fields to feed swine.

"And he would fain have filled his belly with the husks that the swine did eat: and no man gave unto him.

"And when he came to himself, he said, How many hired servants of my father's have bread enough and to spare, and I perish with hunger!

"I will arise and go to my father, and will say unto him, Father, I have sinned against heaven, and before thee,

"And am no more worthy to be called thy son: make me as one of thy hired servants.

"And he arose, and came to his father. But when he was yet a great way off, his father saw him, and had compassion, and ran, and fell on his neck, and kissed him.

"And the son said unto him, Father, I have sinned against heaven, and in thy sight, and am no more worthy to be called thy son.

"But the father said to his servants, Bring forth the best robe, and put it on him; and put a ring on his hand, and shoes on his feet:

"And bring hither the fatted calf, and kill it; and let us eat, and be merry:

"For this my son was dead, and is alive again; he was lost, and is found. And they began to be merry."—Luke 15:11–24.

You've probably seen the same thing I have. Good Christian young people grow up in a good family. They never have a problem with their parents or teachers. They're pliable, compliant and obedient. Theirs is never the voice lifted in rebellion. Theirs is never the hand that is raised in defiance. Theirs are never the feet that stomp out of the room in anger.

Then it's time to leave home, and WHAM. All of the sudden it's as if they never had any Christian training, as if no one ever taught them right from wrong. All of the restrictions and all of the regulations they have lived under are suddenly thrown off. They say, "I'm free—not free to live right or please God or serve the King of Kings. No, I'm free to do whatever I want to do."

One of the most dangerous times in the life of a young person is when he leaves home. I remind parents that it is not simply our job to make sure our children do right; it is our job to teach them to choose to do right. It is not enough to teach them this is right and this is wrong or this is good and this is bad. We must teach them the Bible principles behind those things. If they don't have an appreciation and understanding of the Bible principles behind the rules, there will come a day that the Devil will create a new temptation that will not be on their list.

I think the Devil did that very effectively in the area of movies. Christians who would never darken the door of a theater will buy or rent garbage on a video or DVD. Yet somehow they think that's okay because they didn't go to the theater to see the movie. The video rental store wasn't on the list.

> *One of the most dangerous times in a young person's life is when he leaves home.*

I know a married lady who decided that when she was walking on some of the property her family owned she would wear pants. I'm not recommending that; I'm just telling you what she did. There were a lot of briars and stickers on the property, and she didn't think anyone would be there and see her anyway. Someone did see her, and they called her a harlot because she wore pants.

Now I'm not in favor of women wearing pants, but there is a Bible definition of harlotry, and it has nothing to do with a woman's just wearing pants! When you say something, make sure it is true. That helps people believe it more. Your message is more credible if you tell the truth instead of just saying something that sounds right.

But that same family who got all over the young lady because she wore pants on her private property popped an R-rated video with nudity in it into their VCR and watched that. Now I don't mean to be unkind, but that's idiotic! Why did they do that? The problem was that while women

71

wearing pants was on their list of things that are wrong, watching naked women on the TV screen at home was not on their list.

I hope it will not surprise you to hear that I believe it grieved the Spirit of God a lot more when the family watched nudity on that video than it did when that lady walked across private property in a pair of pants. If they had known the principles rather than the rules, they would have known God was against indecency and immodesty in any setting.

I left home when I was fifteen years old. I didn't run away to join the circus or work in a carnival—I ran away to Bob Jones Academy! That was the extent of my rebellion. I couldn't wait to get there. I thought once I was there, my mother wouldn't be telling me when to get up anymore. She wouldn't be telling me when to go to bed. She wouldn't be telling me how to clean my room. She wouldn't be telling me how to dress. She wouldn't be telling me how much homework I had to do. I couldn't wait to get out from under all the rules and regulations I had at home!

So I went to Bob Jones Academy. I stayed in the same dorms as the college kids. Just as they were, I was required to get up every morning at 6:55 A.M. and go to bed every night at 11:00 P.M. I was required to do a room job. Every day I had to clean the sink and the mirror, dust the furniture, mop the floor or empty the trash. I was even required to make my bed.

At Bob Jones Academy, unless you had a B average, you had to go to study hall and sit in a classroom from 7:00 until 9:30 four nights a week. I had never worked so hard to get a B average in my life. I got the B average, so I got out of study hall. Then I went to the gym or the pool and played every night. The next marking period I ended up right back in study hall because I did not maintain my B average.

I did not leave home to go to a bad place. But even at Bob Jones Academy there were a lot of bad things that could have happened to me. There were young people there that liked to go off and drink. There's a bad crowd and a good crowd no matter where you are.

The transition when a young person leaves home is a dangerous time, but it is going to come. It is supposed to happen. We are not rearing our children for ourselves. We are rearing them to be someone's husband or wife. We are training them to be someone's mother or father. Dr. Ed Johnson, who was a pastor for many years in Rosemount, Minnesota, said, "You don't know what kind of a parent you are until you see how your grandchildren turn out!" Now I want you to notice some lessons about leaving home from the story of the Prodigal Son.

The Tendencies

1. The Tendency to Desire Independence

This young man said, "Dad, let me go; let me loose. Give me the portion of my goods that will someday be coming to me. I know my older brother gets a bigger share than I do, but I'm getting some of it, and I want you to let me have it now. I don't want to wait until the time that you've appointed and the time that you have decided. I want it now. I don't want to wait until you think I'm ready." There is a natural tendency for young people to desire independence.

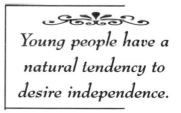

Young people have a natural tendency to desire independence.

This tendency is not inherently wrong. When your daughter gets to sixth or seventh grade, she's not going to want her mother to comb her hair anymore. She's not going to want her parents to tell her how to dress anymore. You can see this tendency even earlier when a child is two and three years old. You want to help them get dressed, and they say, "I can do it myself." I asked my young nephew if he needed help with something once, and he looked at me and said, "I got it, man."

2. The Tendency to Want Independence Before It Is Appropriate

If you are going be a good parent, you have to accept this reality. If you do your job right, there are going to be times when your children think you're a meany. Sometimes they are not going to understand why they can't do something when everyone else does.

There are kids whose parents think it is okay for them to date when they're twelve. I don't care how mature a child is, twelve-year-olds have no business dating! By the way, it should not surprise us that so many young people are losing their purity at an early age. When they've been dating for three years by the time they are fifteen, what's left?

Remember that dating is not in the Bible. I used to think that children were supposed to date. That's what happened at my church when I was growing up. But then I saw what was happening because of it, and I began examining it in the light of reading the Bible. Reading the Bible will mess up a lot of your behaviors, practices, ideas and a whole lot of your theology!

I started teaching our young people that they shouldn't date until they were sixteen, and then it ought to be a double date, and the other couple ought to be Mom and Dad. When young people look at me like I'm crazy, I ask them, "Well, what is it that you would like to do that you wouldn't do in front of your mom and dad?" Allowing children to have independence they are not ready for puts them at a great risk.

The longer you delay the start of the dating process, the better off your kids are. There are studies that show a definite correlation between the age at which young people start dating and when they lose their virginity. Don't give your children the 'portion that will fall to them' before it's time.

3. The Tendency to Want Parents to Pay for Independence

"Dad, would you buy me a car so I can drive it around anywhere I want?" "Mom, I want to be free and live on my own. By the way, here's my laundry. Could you get it done before tomorrow, please?" "Dad, I'm old enough to go to college. I don't want to send you my report card, and I want to make my own decisions, but I'm a little short on money. Could you help me out?"

The Prodigal Son didn't say, "Dad, I think I'd like to go make my own way in the world. I'd like to get a job and start paying for my expenses. I'll pay for the rent on my own apartment and the insurance on my car. I'll buy my gasoline and pay for my dental insurance, my doctor's bills and all of my food and clothing. It's time for me to stand on my own two feet." No, he said, "Give me." He wanted his father to set him up.

4. The Tendency for Parents to Give In to Avoid Confrontation

If you start when your kids are young and tell them, "We're not going to do that dating stuff; you're not going to have a girlfriend or a boyfriend," then I promise you that when they get old, they'll still try to do it. Children will challenge the rules. Even if they know in their heart it's not going to work, they're still going to try, just in case.

I think my daughter Katie could probably mediate the problem in the Middle East! She's a born negotiator. She is always saying to my wife, "Don't make a final decision yet.

What if I get all my piano practice done, all my homework done and get my room cleaned up? What if I do this, and what if I do that?" Now Katie is not a rebel. She doesn't get mad, and she doesn't throw things, but she is still going to test the rules. That is natural.

The problem comes when the parent gets tired of the fussing and the tension. They get tired of the rolled eyes and the slammed door and the stomping out of the room. None of those behaviors are appropriate, and I'm not saying parents should permit it. I'm just telling you what goes on.

> *As long as you live, somebody will be telling you what to do.*

So the parents give in. That is what the father did in the parable of the Prodigal Son. He said, "Here you go. Here's your money." "He divided unto them his living" (Luke 15:12).

5. The Tendency to Separate From the Father

Children often try to assert their independence by striking out on their own. They say, "My parents believe that, but I don't believe that. I am not going to be like my mom and dad." It was not many days after the young man got his money that he was on the road to a far country.

Dr. John R. Rice had a daughter who was engaged to marry what seemed to be a fine young man. The wedding invitations had gone out, the bridal shower had been given, many gifts had been received, and the wedding was just a short time away. The young man said, "I can't wait until I can get you out from all these rules and regulations here. You won't have to live by your daddy's standards anymore." Dr. Rice's daughter looked at that young man and said, "My daddy's standards are my standards. My daddy's beliefs are my beliefs." And she called off the wedding and sent the gifts back.

There are more people like the Prodigal Son than like Dr. Rice's daughter. The natural tendency is for young people to separate from their parents. Though it is a natural tendency, it is wrong and should be guarded against.

6. The Tendency for Young People Who Get Their Freedom to Be Irresponsible

What did the Prodigal Son do when he got his money? He wasted it all on "riotous living." He proved by his behavior that it was way too early for his father to have entrusted him with his inheritance.

I heard a preacher say that the church where he was pastor paid him too much money. (You know that wasn't an independent, fundamental Baptist church!) He said, "I went to the elders and said, 'Look, you pay me too much money.' And they said, 'We know it. We wanted to see what you would do with the surplus. We wanted to see if you would waste it, invest it or give it away.'"

The Prodigal Son wasted his substance in riotous living. Many young people have no real concept of the future. They live as if today were all there was or ever would be. There wouldn't be nearly as many tattoos or weird piercings if people were mature enough to be responsible in light of the future.

7. The Tendency to Reject the Standards and Principles of the Home

It is more likely that your children will reject the standards than the principles, so it is vitally important to teach the principles behind the standards. I would rather have my children keep both, but if they will only stick with one, I would much prefer them to keep the principle but interpret the standard differently than I do.

A preacher said once that you could basically divide the people in church into four groups. The first group believes something because you said it. The second group already believed what you said and joined you because you agreed with them. The third group weighs what you say to see whether or not they believe it. The fourth group doesn't believe anything you say, but they like to hear you say it. There are people in all four of those groups in every church.

He went on to say that all of your prospects for the first two groups are in the last two groups. His point was that you shouldn't run people off because they don't agree with you. I asked him once which group he preferred. He said the first group, "because they trust you implicitly." I understand his thinking, but I disagree with that philosophy. That kind of thinking is how Jim Jones was able to get nine hundred people to drink poisoned Kool-Aid down in the jungles of South America.

I want the members of our church to be in the third group. The Bible says, "These were more noble than those in Thessalonica, in that they received the word with all readiness of mind, and searched the scriptures daily, whether those things were so" (Acts 17:11). People who weigh things against the Scripture are protected from the errors of thinking that often creep into churches.

I tell the people in our church, "If you think that you can follow me just because you like me, then someday you may follow me into error. But if you follow me as I follow Christ, and if the standard for measuring that is the Word of God, then if something is wrong, you will recognize it and not agree with it." I do my best to rightly divide the Scriptures, but I want people to measure what I say against the Word.

That's why we need to teach our children the Word of

God. If there is one class where I want our children to learn a lot, if there's one class where I want them to go beyond memorizing and really learn to think, if there's one class that I think really is worthy of a disproportionate share of a child's time, it is the Bible class. I want them to know the truth.

I've sat in big conferences where famous preachers were talking, and I wrote down what they said, and right next to it I wrote: "not biblical." I didn't fight those preachers; I didn't get up and walk out. They were right about most things, and I don't believe anybody is going to be absolutely perfect. But I am not going to follow anyone where they aren't absolutely following the Word of God.

If you teach your children the principles, you'll come closer to having them follow the Word of God after they leave home. I'd rather have someone disagree with me on the application of a principle but agree with the principle than have somebody who just does something because I say they should.

8. The Tendency Not to Consider the Consequences

Young people just don't think about the future very often. They may think about "when I get a car" or "when I get married" or "when I get out of the house" or "when I have money," but they don't think about the future in the terms of what a particular action will produce in their future.

When I was twenty, I didn't think about what I was going to do when I was fifty. Young people don't usually think about long-term consequences. Young people don't say very often, "I had better not go out with you tonight, because I have this test coming up, and I haven't studied very well. I need to pass the class. If I don't pass the class, I'm not going to graduate; and if I don't graduate, then I'd have to stay an extra year or go to summer school. So I'd really better study for this test." They almost never think like that.

The Prodigal Son didn't think about what was going to happen to him when he was broke. He never said, "What's going to happen to me when I don't have anything to eat and Daddy's a long way away and my family is not here and all these people around me are really just strangers that like me because of my money?" As a result, he ended up in a pigpen.

9. The Tendency to Turn to the World for Help

Do you know where the young man went when he got in trouble? He went to a pigpen. He didn't go home at first. He took a job feeding pigs—which were unclean animals for the Jews. There could be no more degrading a responsibility, no more unpleasant a task than feeding the pigs! But that's what he did. In fact, he was so desperate that he was coveting the pig's food!

Many times parents assume that when things get a little tough, the child will come back. Usually they don't come back until they have spent some time in the pigpen. That's why you had better be careful about letting them go too soon. Teach them the principles that will equip them to live right before they leave home.

Give them the why behind the what. Most importantly, give them the Who behind it. Behind every policy, there ought to be a principle. Behind every principle, there ought to be a Person we're trying to please—the Lord Jesus Christ. Parents, you will save your children and yourself a world of heartache if you will prepare them for a God-pleasing and God-honoring life before they leave your home.

The Trouble

Why does this happen? Why do young people grow up in a good home and do right as long as the parents are there, but then when the restraints are gone they go an entirely different direction?

In the Old Testament, we read about this pattern in the history of the children of Israel. Joshua led them across the Jordan River and into the Promised Land, and after they conquered the Canaanites, he divided up that land and gave them their inheritance. After Joshua died, the children of Israel kept serving God—for a while. The Bible says that they served God all the days of Joshua and all the days of the elders that outlived Joshua, who had seen the works that God had done. But when that generation was gone, the people turned away from God.

1. They Have a Wrong Purpose

I sometimes ask young people, "Why do you want to leave home?" I have never yet had someone reply, "I desire to be a drunkard. I want to be a drug addict. I want to make my life a mess and get all kinds of diseases. I want to have children out of wedlock. I want to get married and have it end in terrible tragedy and divorce. That's my goal for my life." Yet though they don't say that, the sad reality is that some of them do just that.

Why does that happen? Often it happens because young people leave home for the wrong reasons.

Sometimes young people want to leave home because of themselves. There is a built-in human tendency to resist and rebel against authority. Nobody likes to be told what to do.

What happens when people see a sign that says "Wet Paint"? They reach out and touch it to see if it's wet. Can I tell you something? Being able to do your own thing is the wrong reason to leave home. Getting to be in charge of your life and have things the way you want them is the wrong reason to leave home.

When I was an assistant pastor, I did what the preacher said. I didn't cause him trouble. I didn't talk about him behind his back. When I was called to First Baptist Church of Bridgeport, there were some people who indicated they were interested in moving their membership. I told them not to. I wanted to do what was right toward the authority God had placed in my life.

I've heard it said so many times: "I just want to be free." Fallen man resists being told what to do. We don't want any restraints. Young people don't want to be told when to get up, when to go to bed, what to wear, what to watch and what they can have out of the refrigerator. They want to be free, but that is a wrong motive to leave home.

Sometimes young people want to leave home because they want to follow their flesh. The restraints that Mom and Dad have put in place to keep children from sin are the things that bother the children the most. But life is not about choosing for yourself; it's about choosing for the Saviour. It's not about being free; it's about being faithful. It's not about satisfying the flesh; it's about satisfying the Father in Heaven.

If you are eager to leave for the wrong reasons, you are probably going to make a mess of things. If you are looking for an opportunity to satisfy the desires of your flesh, you can be certain that the Devil will see to it that you get that chance. When the Prodigal Son got to the far country, he didn't have to look hard to find places to waste his substance. He found exactly the opportunities to sin that he left home to find.

2. They Have the Wrong Perspective

You probably remember hearing about the young man

who said, "I am sick and tired of being told what to do. I'm tired of my mother. She tells me when to get up, how to dress and when to go to bed. She's always fussing at me about my posture. I am going to run away and join the Marines!" That's a young man without a good perspective on life.

The truth is that as long as you live, somebody will be telling you what to do. I don't care who you are or what you do. President Bush has more restrictions on him than any of us. He can't get out and go to the grocery store. He has far less discretion over his schedule than most of us do. He can't walk down a public street. He can't go to a mall. If he wants to go someplace on vacation, it takes dozens of Secret Service people days to prepare to block everything off and keep him safe.

There isn't anyone in the world who is absolutely free. There isn't anybody that doesn't have someone telling him what to do in at least some part of his life. The Prodigal Son thought, *I'm tired of Daddy's house. I'm tired of the restrictions. I'm tired of the rules and regulations and requirements. I want out of here!* He thought living in freedom would be better than the father's house.

> *Life is not about choosing for yourself; it's about choosing for the Saviour. It's not about being free; it's about being faithful. It's not about satisfying the flesh; it's about satisfying the Father.*

He was wrong. The worst day in his father's house was better than his best day in the pigpen. When he was under the rule of his father, he was better off than when he was doing his own thing, wasting all of his money. What he thought would be a good time was a bad time compared to being in the father's house. He had the wrong perspective.

Young people think everything is going to work out fine. They have a hard time considering the consequences and understanding the long-term results of their behavior. And I'm not criticizing; that's just how it is. When you're young, you don't think you'll ever get old. Mickey Mantle, the outstanding baseball player, died of liver failure and complications brought on by years of drinking. He said, "If I had known I was going to live this long, I would have taken better care of myself!" But by then, it was too late.

3. They Have the Wrong Preparation

There is the wrong preparation on the part of parents. Parents need to train their children to be independent. There's a term psychologists use called "codependency." It's not a term used in the Bible, and you don't have to believe it, but I think there's some truth to what they describe. The idea is that some people get into a relationship and depend on each other in an unhealthy way.

For example, the counselor needs to be needed by the counselee, and the counselee needs someone to give him a sense of security and tell him what to do. The counselor needs his ego affirmed by someone wanting his advice, and the counselee needs his insecurity addressed by someone giving him direction for life. Instead of truly helping each other, they get into a never-ending relationship.

My goal isn't to have everyone in our church come to see me for counseling every week. I know some preachers who preach against buying a car without getting the preacher's counsel. There are a lot of people in our church that know more about buying a car than I do. If you want mechanical advice, don't come to me.

I can tell you if the car is started or not. I can tell you

if the turn signals work or not. I can tell you whether or not there appears to be a muffler on there, but I'm no mechanic. If you would like to go buy a car tomorrow, you have to check with God, not with me. My goal isn't to have a bunch of people that have to check with me before they can breathe, before they can dress, before they can date or before they can do anything else. My goal as a pastor is to train people who know how to get their help from God. That way even after I'm dead and gone, they will still make right choices.

Some parents try to hold their children in all the time. They don't want them to grow up. I understand that. Both my daughters promised me when they were little that they wouldn't grow up. They lied to me! Your children are going to grow up, and you should want them to. Do you know what they call someone who never grows up? I don't mean to be unkind or disrespectful, but they call that person retarded. The word *retard* means "to slow down or hold back." It was originally not a pejorative term; it just meant a person's growth was not what it ought to be.

> The most important part of training children is teaching them the principles of the Word of God.

Sometimes parents don't prepare their children for the future. They think that if they put food on the table and clothes in the closet, they have done their job as parent. That is not enough. The future is coming whether or not you like it.

Teach them about money. Start by giving them a little bit of money and see how they spend it. Give them an amount of money and have them make it last for a certain period of time. Plan for the upcoming youth activities and school lunches they have and then see if they have any money left at the end. They need to understand that expression: "having too much month left at the end of the money," and how to keep that from happening.

It wouldn't hurt your daughter to know how to cook. It wouldn't be bad if your son knew how to change the oil, do some basic repairs on a lawn mower or put a washer on a faucet. But more important than any of those skills is being able to figure out what is right and what is wrong. They must know how to take the Bible and use it to decide what they should do in a given situation.

I wanted our girls to get a good education. Krissy worked hard to make sure that they did their homework. When they needed help with studying for a test, we helped them. But far more than wanting them to learn English or history or science, I wanted them to learn the principles of the Word of God. That is the most important part of training them for adulthood.

Sometimes there is also wrong preparation on the part of children. It is difficult to get young people to see things from this perspective. The time to learn how to respond is before you are put to the test. You will not succeed in the Christian life if you wait to decide what to do when a temptation arises.

When our daughters were little, we would ask, "If a boy ever wanted to date you, what would you say?" And they would reply, "Ask Mom and Dad." We would continue, "What if we say no?" The right answer was, "I wouldn't date him." Karissa would usually say, "I'd find someone else!" Then we'd say, "Where would be a really fun place to go on a date?" They would say, "Home to play games with Mom and Dad and the boy."

Then we'd ask, "Would you ever date a boy that wasn't saved? Would you ever date a boy that wasn't a soul winner? Would you ever date a boy who wasn't a Baptist?" They would say, "No." I started doing that when they were three and four. Now I really didn't think my daughters were about to start dating. But I did know that one day some guy would want to date them, and I wanted to get them ready.

The Truths

1. Parents Must Train Their Children

The Prodigal Son's father did not train him. That young man had no idea how to handle money (at least if he had been given teaching he certainly rejected it) or how to take an investment and make something out of it. As a result, he was not prepared to live on his own. Remember too that it is not enough just to tell your children the truth—you need to train them effectively so that they will do what is right.

Suppose you send your dog off to obedience school and when he comes back, you say, "Sit" and the dog just stands there and looks at you. When you say, "Come," the dog stays where it is. And when you say, "Lie down," the dog doesn't do anything. You would tell the dog trainer, "I'm not paying for this." Would you be satisfied if he replied, "I did train him. I put him through the paces. If I've told that dog once I've told him a thousand times, you come when I say come and sit when I say sit." Of course not! If the dog doesn't do what he's told, he's not trained. So parents must train their children. That is, they must bring them to the point of right behavior, not just right knowledge.

2. Children Must Listen to Their Parents

The Bible again and again commands children to listen to their parents. And parents should not be discouraged when it appears that the children are not getting it. You should not feel like a failure or that you are doing something wrong. You are not wasting your time, because there is something that happens in the training process. It may seem like no progress is being made, but there is work being done on the inside that neither the person doing the training nor the person being worked on is fully aware of.

Why did Solomon ask for wisdom when God offered him anything that he wanted? He could have asked for riches, power or long life; instead he chose a wise heart. Solomon made that specific request because David had trained him.

> *"For I was my father's son, tender and only beloved in the sight of my mother.*
>
> *"He taught me also, and said unto me, Let thine heart retain my words: keep my commandments, and live.*
>
> *"Get wisdom, get understanding: forget it not; neither decline from the words of my mouth.*
>
> *"Forsake her not, and she shall preserve thee: love her, and she shall keep thee.*
>
> ***"Wisdom is the principal thing; therefore get wisdom:*** *and with all thy getting get understanding."*—Prov. 4:3–7 (emphasis added).

3. The Fewer Lessons We Learn by Experience, the Better Off We Are

Someone once said, "Experience is a harsh teacher, but some men will learn from no other." Henry Ford said, "The problem with the school of experience is that by the time a man graduates he is too old to work!" It is far better for children to learn from us than from experience.

It is natural for us to want to try things for ourselves. And there are some things that we have to learn by experience, but the fewer lessons you learn by experience, the better. I've been delivered from a life of drunkenness, idolatry, addiction and immorality. I was delivered from all those things before I ever did them! It has in no way hindered my ability to enjoy life that I have been morally pure. It hasn't hurt me a bit!

4. It Is Dangerous to Give a Child Independence Too Early

I have already discussed the importance of teaching your children to make decisions at an early age. Let them make a decision where there is a better choice and a lesser choice, but no evil choice. Don't let them choose between going to church and staying home and watching some program on television.

But let them choose sometime between doing their homework the night before a test and playing Playstation. Say, "You know you have a test tomorrow, and you told me you hadn't studied very much, but if you want to, go ahead and play the game. I think you ought to study, but you can make your own choice." Then when they flunk and they're off the ball team or they have to repeat a class, ask them what they learned.

You need to let them make some mistakes. You need to protect them from terrible mistakes, but it's good to let them do a few things and realize that they don't have much to show for it. So I would suggest you give them freedom in some scenarios where they won't do permanent damage but they will be able to see the consequences of their bad behavior.

It is dangerous to give children independence too early. But it is also dangerous to give children independence too late. If you never let them make a decision, how will they know how to choose? If you never let them suffer the consequences of their behavior, if you always bail them out, when will they learn that there is a price to pay for their choices? You must prepare your children now, because the day is coming (sooner than you think) when they will be leaving home. Make sure they are ready before they do.

6

When Your Children Get in Trouble

For the first ten years of our marriage, we did not have children. During that time, especially after I became a pastor, I began to observe how people reared their children. I saw many things I wanted to copy with my children and many things I wanted to avoid.

I think in some ways it was a blessing from the Lord for our children to be delayed. I was probably a better father later in life than I would have been earlier. God knows what He is doing. We prayed for years to have children, and in His perfect timing, He gave us two wonderful daughters.

One of the things I noticed over the years is that the biggest experts on child rearing are married people who have no children! Those people are really smart. They always know what everyone else should do. In fact, I think we should require that all books on children be written by these folks, since they are the ones who know so much. I have also noticed that the greatest experts on teenagers are parents of toddlers and grade-school children. They are certain that their little angels will never turn out like *those* kids.

I believe that every parent (as opposed to these experts) would tell you there are at least some areas in which their children need help. Because our children are born with the same sin nature we have, they will do things that are wrong. Whether these failures are large or small, it is important for parents to understand how to respond properly.

The Responsibility to Train

1. The Prescription

The Bible tells us what our job as parents is. One of our primary responsibilities is to teach our children what is right. Romans 16:19 says, "For your obedience is come abroad unto all men. I am glad therefore on your behalf: but yet I would have you wise unto that which is good, and simple concerning evil." The word "simple" means to be unaware.

Parents have a responsibility to protect their children. I have heard parents say, "Well, they need to know what the real world is like. If you keep them sheltered, they won't know what to do when they go out on their own. You're raising greenhouse Christians!" That philosophy may sound good to some, but it contradicts the Bible. God does not want your children (or you for that matter) to be exposed to evil in order to learn how to handle it. We are to be separated from the world, not trying to see how involved with it we can be (Jas. 1:27).

When I was a boy, we lived on Main Street in Perry, Michigan. Now if I took my toy car outside to play and decided that the paved road was better than the grass because the car would run better, what would my mother do? She did not give me a discourse on the Department of Transportation. She did not explain the laws of physics to me to describe what would happen if a car hit me. She told me to get out of the road. It was not safe for me to be there.

In the backyard of the parsonage of the Perry Baptist Church, there was a weeping willow tree. The poet said, "The branches bend down to the ground, like falling tears." That's not the reason it's called a weeping willow tree; it's called that because of the response of a child when one of those branches is broken off and used by his mother as a switch! (It is possible that there might be a connection between my memories of being told not to play in the road and that willow tree.)

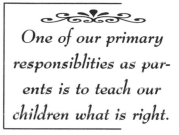

One of our primary responsiblities as parents is to teach our children what is right.

Why did my mother spank me? She didn't want me to be hurt by playing in the road. She was trying to protect me.

There is a tendency to let down our guard in protection as our children get older. I know parents of teenagers who never ask who else is going to be at the house where their children are going or if they're going to go anyplace else while they're out. The responsibility for protection does not end on the thirteenth birthday.

Parents have a responsibility to correct their children. Proverbs 22:15 says, "Foolishness is bound in the heart of a child; but the rod of correction shall drive it far from him." Please notice what this verse is saying. It is not school that corrupts children. It is not the neighbor's kid who teaches them how to lie. There can be evil influences on your children, but their nature is corrupt because of sin. It starts in their heart.

You cannot rely on their getting better on their own. In fact, Proverbs 29:15 says, "The rod and reproof give wisdom: but a child left to himself bringeth his mother to shame." Instead you must take steps to point out, punish and stop the bad behavior of your children. If you do not correct them, you are heading for trouble.

From time to time I preach in Christian school chapels across the country. Often I speak to the kids about the responsibility of their parents to correct them. It is part of our fleshly nature and the folly bound in our hearts to resist correction. I sometimes ask them how many still suck their thumbs. Nobody has ever yet admitted it. Then I point out that it was their parents who got them to quit doing that. They needed correction then, and they still need it as teens.

Parents have a responsibility to perfect their children. Ephesians 6:4 says, "And, ye fathers, provoke not your children to wrath: but bring them up in the nurture and admonition of the Lord." The word "nurture" means "tutoring"; the word "admonition" means "to call attention to" and refers to a mild rebuke or warning. Both are essential. You must not only warn them when they do wrong, you must build them up so that they will do right.

Parents need to train children to do right. My friend Dr. Curtis Hutson told about a time when his son, Tony, didn't clean up his room. His wife said, "I taught him better than that." Dr. Hutson replied, "No, you *told* him. If you had taught him, he would have cleaned his room." There is a big difference between telling and training. Many parents have told their children to do right, but they do not insist on proper performance. It can become a contest of wills. As the process drags on, the parents can give up, but the results are disastrous for the children.

In this context, perfecting your children means helping them get to the place where they are doing the things you have been teaching them. Of course it does not mean they will be perfect; the biblical use of the word carries the sense of completion—having everything that is needed.

2. The Principle

Proverbs 22:6 says, "Train up a child in the way he

should go: and when he is old, he will not depart from it."
Now I know that there is a lot of debate over the meaning
of this verse. I have noticed over the years that people's
opinion of this verse is often determined by how well their
children turned out. Proverbs are general principles; things
that are generally true. They are not absolute promises. All
of the Proverbs are the Word of God, they are true, they are
valid, and they work. But we must compare Scripture with
Scripture.

The Bible also says, "So then every one of us shall give
account of himself to God" (Rom. 14:12). We as Baptists
believe in the priesthood of the believer and individual
responsibility. Nobody answers to God for you except you.
You can't blame your failures on anything or anyone else.

Some people grow up in a
good home with good training
and still willfully and deliber-
ately choose to do wrong and
go away from God. I have a
friend who went to a
Christian school with two
boys from the same family.
Today, one of them is a
Christian school principal; the

All of us will give account for what we did to God. Don't blame anyone else for mistakes you make.

other is serving a life sentence for murder. As a general rule
though, if a child is trained to do right, he will continue to
do so. If that were not true, God would not have placed it
in the Bible.

It does make a difference how you rear your children. It
may sometimes seem like it is not working. Many parents
become discouraged and stop trying. That is a mistake. I
went to Bob Jones for five years—one year of high school
and four years of college. There were things that I disagreed
with while I was there. Over time I came to agree with

many of their positions, especially when I got out into the ministry and saw how things worked in the real world.

Discipline, truth and the repetition of the Word of God have a powerful effect. Years ago a preacher told a story about a boy working on a farm. The farmer told him to take a sieve down to the creek, fill it with water and then bring it back. Of course by the time the boy returned, all the water had dripped out through the holes. The boy said, "It's empty." The farmer replied, "Yes, but now it's clean!"

3. The Prohibition

When God gives a negative command in the Bible it is to call our attention to something that is especially important to avoid. We've already looked at Ephesians 6:4, but now I want to call your attention to the first part of the verse: "And, ye fathers, provoke not your children to wrath: but bring them up in the nurture and admonition of the Lord."

> *Because they are sinners, all children will sometimes do wrong.*

What does it mean to provoke your children to wrath? Matthew Henry says it refers to a person who by continued haranguing becomes to the child an enemy instead of a friend. Whatever you do, don't provoke your child to wrath. This does not mean that your children will never be upset with a decision you make or a discipline you enforce.

You must be sure that the discipline is given in love. If you discipline out of anger, frustration or shame, you are not training your children, rather, you are provoking them. Angry children do not follow their parents; they rebel against them and against everything they stand for and believe. As a parent, you are commanded by God not to provoke them to wrath. Never discipline your children in anger. It is far better to wait an hour or two (assuming they are not doing something life-threatening) until you are in control of yourself and can discipline properly, than it is to do it in the heat of the moment.

I remember my father sitting down across from me when I had done something wrong. He would review the situation, making me tell him what I had done wrong. He would ask me questions to determine that I knew why what I had done was wrong. Then he would ask me what the punishment for that offense was supposed to be. I hated that question. By disciplining in that way, he made it difficult for me to blame him for the punishment. Instead, I accepted responsibility for what I had done.

The Response to Trouble

Because they are sinners, children will sometimes do wrong, even if they are properly trained. So what should parents do when that happens? I want to give you two examples from Scripture and then some practical applications to help you answer that question.

1. Example of a Spiritual Leader

Eli was the top leader in the nation of Israel. He was the one people looked to for both spiritual and secular guidance. He was the mouthpiece of God. He was the representative of God who offered the sacrifices that were a type of the Lamb of God who would come to pay for the sins of the world. Yet his sons did not know the Lord.

The Charges. *Eli's sons desecrated the sacrifice.*

"Wherefore the sin of the young men was very great before the LORD: *for men abhorred the offering of the* LORD*"*—I Sam. 2:17.

God's plan of provision for the priests was that they would receive part of the sacrifices for their own food. But rather than be content with their allotted portion, Hophni and Phinehas took the best cuts of meat for themselves. They took something that was supposed to be a joyous time, as the people of God brought their offerings, and turned it into an occasion to satisfy their appetites.

Things got so bad that people hated going to the tabernacle and giving their sacrifices. We've seen some spiritual leaders in our day defile the testimony of God. We've seen spiritual leaders leave the ministry in disgrace because of moral or financial sins.

Eli's sons defiled the tabernacle.

"Now Eli was very old, and heard all that his sons did unto all Israel; and how they lay with the women that assembled at the door of the tabernacle of the congregation"— I Sam. 2:22.

They turned a place of holiness into a place of wickedness. They took a sacred place and turned it into a sensual place.

These two young men misused their position as spiritual leaders to take advantage of women who came to worship God. I believe those women were guilty for participating in immorality, but the greatest fault and responsibility rested on the sons of Eli.

Eli dishonored God.

"Wherefore kick ye at my sacrifice and at mine offering, which I have commanded in my habitation; and honourest thy sons above me, to make yourselves fat with the chiefest of all the offerings of Israel my people?"—I Sam. 2:29.

When Eli had to make a choice between doing what was right and protecting his children, he chose his sons over God.

A leader who allows people under him to continue in wickedness brings dishonor to the name of God. Most people do not like confrontation. It is easier to let things slide than to deal with a problem. Eli talked to his sons, but he did not insist that they either change their wicked behavior or he would remove them from their position.

Eli was delinquent in his responsibility.

> *"For I have told him that I will judge his house for ever for the iniquity which he knoweth; because his sons made themselves vile, and he restrained them not"*—I Sam. 3:13.

Eli's sons were grown men. They were responsible for their own choices and conduct. But as the priest, Eli had a responsibility to force them to either change or leave.

Neither leaders nor parents will always see their followers or children do what is right. But they always have a responsibility to deal with the problem. Eli could have stopped his sons from stealing the sacrifices and committing

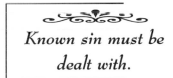

Known sin must be dealt with.

immorality at the tabernacle by removing them from the position that they were abusing. We cannot keep them from ever doing wrong, but we must deal with the sin when it becomes known.

The Chastisement. First Samuel 3:11 says, "And the LORD said to Samuel, Behold, I will do a thing in Israel, at which both the ears of every one that heareth it shall tingle." I love the descriptive language God uses here. The punishment God was going to bring on Eli and his family would cause people to sit up and listen with both ears wide open!

God declared to Samuel that because of Eli's failure to deal with the sins of his sons, the entire family would be judged:

> *"For I have told him that I will judge his house for ever*

for the iniquity which he knoweth; because his sons made themselves vile, and he restrained them not.

"And therefore I have sworn unto the house of Eli, that the iniquity of Eli's house shall not be purged with sacrifice nor offering for ever."—I Sam. 3:13, 14.

Eli's descendants would never again be trusted with the privilege and responsibility of the priesthood. It is a serious thing to fail as a leader of God's people. James highlighted this same truth: "My brethren, be not many masters, knowing that we shall receive the greater condemnation" (Jas. 3:1).

In a single day, Hophni and Phinehas were killed in battle; and when Eli heard the news, he fell over backward and broke his neck. Just as God had promised, the judgment was swift, sure and final. Eli failed completely when it came to dealing with the trouble in his sons' lives.

2. Example of a Secular Leader

David repeatedly had to deal with problems with his sons. On three distinct occasions, we see how he dealt with his sons and what the result was in each case.

David indulged Adonijah. Before David died, he designated Solomon to be his heir. But that choice did not meet with unanimous approval. Adonijah, who was David's fourth son and older than Solomon, decided that he should be king instead. So before David was even dead, he tried to set himself up as king over the people.

"Then Adonijah the son of Haggith exalted himself, saying, I will be king: and he prepared him chariots and horsemen, and fifty men to run before him.

"And his father had not displeased him at any time in saying, Why hast thou done so? and he also was a very goodly man; and his mother bare him after Absalom."—I Kings 1:5, 6.

Adonijah might well have become king except for the intervention of Nathan and Bathsheba with David. His effort failed, and Solomon took the throne. It is fascinating to see what the Bible says here about David's parenting. He had never called Adonijah to account for his conduct. Adonijah could do anything that he wanted.

There are people advising parents today who encourage them not ever to make their children unhappy. There are movements in the educational community to abolish grades. Some schools will not let the children play games where they keep score to make sure there aren't any winners and losers. Children need discipline, guidelines and absolute standards in their lives.

Because David indulged Adonijah, he became selfish. If you are used to getting everything you want when you're little, you think you should have everything you want when you're older. It is not uncommon for the youngest child in a family to be spoiled because he is treated differently by the parents than the older children were. You are a bad parent if you never say no to your children.

> *You are not a bad parent if you say no to your child; you are a bad parent if you never say no to your child.*

David was indifferent to Absalom. David's refusal to deal with Amnon's sin in raping Tamar (Absalom's sister) made Absalom angry. So he waited two years and then arranged for Amnon's murder. He fled to his mother's homeland and stayed there for three years. Finally David let Absalom come home, but he refused to allow him to come back to the palace.

"So Joab arose and went to Geshur, and brought Absalom to Jerusalem.

"And the king said, Let him turn to his own house, and let him not see my face. So Absalom returned to his own house, and saw not the king's face."—II Sam. 14:23, 24.

Two more years went by without Absalom's being allowed into David's presence.

Because David was indifferent to him, Absalom became seditious. Though David finally allowed Absalom to return to Jerusalem, he never did fully forgive him. Their relationship was never restored. I counseled a man once who had been unfaithful to his wife thirty years before. They had stayed married, but she never let him forget it. They never had a sweet and happy relationship again. He said, "I wish she had gone ahead and divorced me."

Because of his bitterness over David's indifference, Absalom mounted a rebellion against him. He gathered an army and tried to take over the throne. Parents should not be surprised if the children they have no time for turn against them. David wept when he learned that Absalom had been killed, but he was to blame.

David instructed Solomon. Although David had failed with other children, he spent the time with Solomon to give him the skills to be a good king over the people. Among other things, he instructed Solomon on the importance of wisdom. "Only the LORD give thee wisdom and understanding, and give thee charge concerning Israel, that thou mayest keep the law of the LORD thy God" (I Chron. 22:12).

Because David instructed Solomon, Solomon became spiritual. He became a seeker after God. Now it is true that Solomon did not stay spiritual all of his life, but David started him out in the right direction. There is no substitute for parental instruction. I thank God for every faithful Sunday school and Christian school teacher. I thank God for every faithful youth worker and pastor. But none of them can fully play the role that God has designed for parents to fill. The primary training agency always has been and always will be the home.

Parents are meant to be the primary instructors and role models for the children. That requires a huge investment of time and effort. There are no shortcuts or substitutes for extended, intensive and personal teaching. Day after day, time after time, you must teach your children. I believe that discipleship is a Bible command, but the most important discipling you will ever do is that of your own children.

3. Exhortations to Parents

Teach the truth before your children get into trouble. Don't wait until they're already doing something wrong. It is much harder to convince them to give up something for which they've developed an appetite. As Benjamin Franklin said, "An ounce of prevention is worth a pound of cure."

Teach them to obey first and seek an explanation later. I often told my daughters, "First we obey, and then we explain." Children should never be given the idea that everything is subject to negotiation. Obedience protects children, and they need to learn it at an early age. It is not wrong to explain the why behind the what in fact it is important, but that is not the first priority.

Caution them to expect unfair treatment. Life will not be fair, and there is no reason to teach your kids to expect it to be. Prepare them for things to go wrong and to be treated wrongly. Do not give them an expectation of entitlement. They need to know how to respond properly when they are mistreated.

Demonstrate grief for their sin rather than embarrassment for your shame. When children do something wrong, parents are often more upset for their own reputation. While children do reflect on the parents by their

103

conduct, the reason to discipline them is to keep them from doing wrong.

Listen to their side. When your children get in trouble, ask them what happened. That does not mean that you should believe everything they say. Compare it against the evidence. As President Reagan used to say, "Trust, but verify." But do not punish a child until you know what they have to say regarding what happened.

Ask questions and avoid accusations. Sometimes children get in trouble because what they did was misunderstood. Listen carefully to what they have to say. Questions stir the conscience; accusations harden the will. This is the pattern God established with Adam and Eve in the Garden of Eden. He knew the answers already, thus He questioned them not to acquire information but to stir the conscience.

Support the position of authority even when you can't support the practice. Teachers, coaches and pastors will sometimes make mistakes. In those cases, you need not to undermine their authority with your children, even if you don't agree with what they have done. Teach your children the truth that all authority is ordained by God.

About twenty years ago, a young man from a godly family was expelled from the Christian school operated by his church. Though he disagreed with the punishment, his father said, "We are not going to leave the church. We will not attack those we feel wronged our son. We will accept this situation as from the hand of God." The young man was readmitted the following year and finished school. Then he went off to Bible college and for many years has been a successful assistant pastor—at that same church!

Determine to grow spiritually yourself through the experience. It is difficult to see your children go through trouble, but in addition to helping them through it, look on it as an opportunity to draw closer to God yourself. As you humble yourself, you can learn from trials and tribulations.

Look for any areas that you need to strengthen. When your child gets in trouble, evaluate the example you have set for them. It may be that their problem is a result of a weakness in your life. Accept responsibility for areas in which you have failed to model the right pattern of behavior and work to change your own life for the better.

Encourage your child to grow spiritually through the experience. Help them to look at their problem as an opportunity to grow closer to God. Show them God's plan for us when things go wrong and we respond properly (1 Peter 2:18–21). It's interesting to me that this is the only thing we find in Scripture for which God thanks us.

Look for any areas that your child needs to strengthen. Find verses of Scripture that deal with their specific areas of weakness and have them memorize them. Use Bible examples to help them find ways they can become stronger as Christians. Make sure they understand the connection between that weakness in their character and the problem they are experiencing.

See the hand of God in the situation. Even if everyone involved in a situation is intentionally being unfair and unkind, God is still able to use that for good. Joseph suffered unjustly, but "God meant it unto good" (Gen. 50:20). God used the bad behavior of others to bring His purpose to fulfillment in Joseph's life.

Determine not to go backward in any area of your Christian life. Do not stop going to church, reading your Bible or working for the Lord. Failure in one area of the Christian life does not mean you should or must fail in others. Do not allow what happens to your child to drive a wedge between you and God.

Do not try to justify yourself or your children to others. I

105

have learned over the years that it is almost always a waste of time to try to explain what happened to people who are not involved in the situation. If you have made things right with God, take your licks, pay your dues and then just smile and go on. If you try to justify yourself, you end up sounding like you are whining.

Give your children hope for the future. When they get in trouble, let them know that it is not the end. They still have a life and a future, and God still can use them. He will bring good out of it if we respond appropriately. Many times children feel worthless when they have failed. They need to know that you love them and that you believe in their future.

7

Divorce

"And this have ye done again, covering the altar of the LORD with tears, with weeping, and with crying out, inso much that he regardeth not the offering any more, or receiveth it with good will at your hand.

"Yet ye say, Wherefore? Because the LORD hath been witness between thee and the wife of thy youth, against whom thou hast dealt treacherously: yet is she thy companion, and the wife of thy covenant.

"And did not he make one? Yet had he the residue of the spirit. And wherefore one? That he might seek a godly seed. Therefore take heed to your spirit, and let none deal treacherously against the wife of his youth.

"For the LORD, the God of Israel, saith that he hateth putting away: for one covereth violence with his garment, saith the LORD of hosts: therefore take heed to your spirit, that ye deal not treacherously."—Mal. 2:13-16.

Divorce is not the unpardonable sin. Some churches treat it like it is. They treat people who have been divorced as if they are second-class citizens. God is not in favor of divorce separating what He has joined together. "From the beginning it was not so," Jesus said (Matt. 19:8). But divorce is a reality. Even if the divorce was outside the will of God, that sin is just as forgivable as any other.

The statistics on divorce in society as a whole are not markedly different from those of people who call themselves Christians. Now of course we realize that not everyone, especially in our world today, who identifies himself as a believer is truly saved. Still, those of us who know the Lord and have the Spirit of God living within should be more committed to a marriage that is strong and lasting.

Everyone who comes into the church starts from where they are. Many people were divorced before they got saved. Many others have a divorce in their past but have sought forgiveness for their part in it and are striving to do the best they can going forward. We should not hold people accountable for what has already been forgiven.

> *God does not hate divorced people.*

In the Bible there are only two areas of ministry in which divorced people cannot serve—being a pastor and being a deacon. I believe that any other position within the church should be open to people regardless of whether or not they have been divorced. Some churches refuse to allow divorced people to teach Sunday school classes or serve in other areas, but that kind of prohibition goes beyond what the Scripture requires. God hates divorce. God does not hate divorced people.

The Problem in Society

1. The Problem Is Invasive

There are fewer people in America today in their first marriage than there are in a subsequent marriage. Each year there are half as many people getting divorced as there are getting married. Seventy-five percent of the people who get divorced get remarried within a short period of time. Sixty percent of second marriages end in divorce. Seventy-two percent of third marriages end in divorce. Ninety-three percent of fourth marriages end in divorce.

2. The Problem Is Increasing

The number of divorced people in America more than quadrupled from 1970 (4.3 million) to 1996 (18.3 million). In 1997, 255 couples got divorced every day. Children who come from a divorced home are fifty percent more likely to get divorced themselves.

3. The Problem Is Infectious

If you are divorced, you are at a much higher risk for depression and suicide. More children live in single-parent families because of divorce than because of births out of

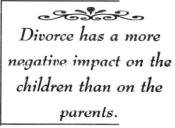

Divorce has a more negative impact on the children than on the parents.

wedlock. Half of all children will witness the breakup of their parents' marriage. Half of those children (twenty-five percent of all children) will witness the breakup of their parents' second marriage. Sociologists who study the issue report that divorce has a more negative impact on a child than does the death of a parent.

The Position of Scripture

There are four primary viewpoints that people in churches take when it comes to the matter of divorce. Let's briefly look at each along with the scriptural support that those who take each view use for their position.

1. There Are No Grounds for Divorce

The people who hold this view cite Luke 16:18 which says, "Whosoever putteth away his wife, and marrieth another, committeth adultery: and whosoever marrieth her that is put away from her husband committeth adultery." They say that any divorce is adultery. That position would be acceptable if that were the only verse in the Bible on the subject. However there are other verses that have to be considered as well.

2. Divorce Is Acceptable for Fornication, but There Are No Grounds for Remarriage

These people quote Jesus in Matthew 19:9 where He said, "And I say unto you, Whosoever shall put away his wife, except it be for fornication, and shall marry another, committeth adultery: and whoso marrieth her which is put away doth commit adultery." Under the Old Testament law, divorce was easy to get. There was no recourse for a woman whose husband wanted to get rid of her. If he said "I divorce you" three times, the marriage was over.

The Pharisees questioned Jesus about this practice, looking as they often did for an opportunity to trap Him. Jesus responded by citing the original design God had for marriage. Marriage is God's idea, and He did not mean for it to be divided by anyone. Moses made an allowance for divorce because the people had hard and stubborn hearts. However that was not part of God's original plan.

This passage is the most extensive teaching Jesus gave on the subject of divorce. Some people read what Jesus said in this passage and conclude that, while divorce is acceptable in this one case, there is no provision for the divorced person to remarry. I believe this position, which is held by many well-meaning people, misses an important truth.

3. Divorce Is Acceptable on Grounds of Fornication, and, in That Case, Remarriage Is Acceptable as Well

God never prefers divorce, and His will is for the partners to be reconciled and restored. My friend Dr. Curtis

Hutson told me he would not remarry a divorced person if they had a living, unremarried spouse. He did not want to close the door on a possible reconciliation.

I believe what Jesus taught in Matthew 19 is that fornication provides an exception to the unbreakable nature of marriage. Thus it is acceptable, although not required, to divorce because of fornication; and, in such a case, it is also acceptable to remarry. Understanding this teaching of Jesus requires that we understand what He was talking about when He referred to fornication.

Some people teach that fornication refers only to unfaithfulness during the betrothal period. In Jewish culture, the man and woman were espoused (like Joseph and Mary), sometimes for a lengthy period, before the wedding. They were promised to each other. Those who teach this limit fornication to breaking that betrothal. I do not believe that position can be supported from Scripture.

The word translated "fornication" is the Greek word *pornea*, from which we get the word *pornography*. It refers to much more than unfaithfulness during the betrothal period, as it is used throughout the Bible. There are some places where it could apply to the betrothal period, but there are many more places where it is clearly referring to other contexts.

For example, when the Jerusalem Council met to consider what instructions to give the Gentile Christians, they wrote: "That ye abstain from meats offered to idols, and from blood, and from things strangled, and from fornication: from which if ye keep yourselves, ye shall do well. Fare ye well" (Acts 15:29). Did they want to tell the new Christians to be morally pure only during their betrothals? Of course not.

Fornication is a broad term that refers to various kinds of sexual impurity. Adultery is a subset of fornication and generally refers to immorality between married people. So what did Jesus mean when he allowed divorce in the case of fornication? I believe He was talking about one partner in the marriage (after the marriage) being unfaithful.

Adultery is a sin with special consequences. Proverbs 6:32, 33 says

> *"But whoso committeth adultery with a woman lacketh understanding: he that doeth it destroyeth his own soul.*
>
> *"A wound and dishonour shall he get; and his reproach shall not be wiped away."*

This does not mean that adultery is a more heinous sin than others, but that the destructive effects are greater and longer lasting.

In the Old Testament, the penalty for adultery was death. That is why the Pharisees brought the woman taken in adultery to Jesus in John 8. They were tempting him to see if He would enforce the letter of the law. The penalty was death by stoning, but the stoning was to be carried out by the witnesses. Thus Jesus said for those who were innocent to cast the first stones at her.

So in the Old Testament the innocent spouse whose partner committed adultery was always able to remarry— the guilty party was dead! In the New Testament era, we are under grace rather than under the law. Adultery is not a capital offense in our country. But why would God under grace not extend the same opportunity to remarry that the innocent spouse had under the law? I believe that He does and that therefore when a marriage is dissolved because of divorce, the innocent party is free to remarry.

Adultery breaks the one-flesh relationship. The one-flesh relationship is the very essence of marriage. Jesus said,

> *"For this cause shall a man leave father and mother, and shall cleave to his wife: and they twain shall be one flesh?*

> *"Wherefore they are no more twain, but one flesh. What therefore God hath joined together, let not man put asunder."*—Matt. 19:5, 6.

Adultery undermines the very heart of the marriage relationship.

Refusing to allow biblically divorced people to remarry creates a church discipline issue. If people who are divorced and get remarried are committing adultery, it would be wrong to allow anyone who is remarried to hold any position in the church or even to be a church member, because they would be living in sin and would be subject to church discipline. Everyone I know who holds the position that remarriage is wrong still allows people who are remarried to keep coming to church. That is not consistent.

God divorced Israel. Jeremiah 3:8 says, "And I saw, when for all the causes whereby backsliding Israel committed adultery I had put her away, and given her a bill of divorce; yet her treacherous sister Judah feared not, but went and played the harlot also." For hundreds of years, God sent prophets and judges to call the people back to Himself. They refused again and again. If you believe there should never be divorce for any reason, you are saying God violates what the Bible teaches.

4. Divorce Is Acceptable for Many Causes, and Remarriage Is Permitted

Some people say divorce is acceptable if the marriage was not "in the Lord." They cite I Corinthians 7:39 for this, but that verse simply teaches that Christians should only marry Christians, not that they should get divorced if they did not marry a believer.

Some argue for divorce on the grounds of incompatibility or desertion. Those who add to the Bible's reasons for divorce are generally arguing (although they may not be willing to admit it) for divorce for any reason at all. They keep expanding it beyond what the Bible says in an attempt to get the result they want.

The Prescription for the Suffering

1. Recognize That While Divorce Is Permitted, It Is Not Preferred

God allows divorce in the case of fornication, but divorce is not His plan. Adultery does not require divorce. I believe that the injured party should try to restore the relationship if it is possible to do so. Divorce is never the best, but sometimes it does happen despite a person's best efforts.

2. God Gets More Glory From Reconciliation and Rebuilding Than From Divorce and Dissolution

I know some preachers who run off people anytime they have a problem with them. Most of them have very small churches. It is far better to work to resolve disputes and disagreements. When a couple who have great problems work to rebuild a strong relationship, it is a powerful testimony to the power of God, and it brings Him glory.

> *The injured party should try to restore the relationship.*

3. Do Not Be the One to End the Marriage or the One to End the Possibility of Reconciliation

While some of the people I have counseled ended up getting a divorce, I have never counseled anyone to do so. I encourage people to wait and see what God will do. If the marriage is going to be permanently broken, let it be the other person who does it rather than you. In our society, divorce is usually not avoidable if one person insists on

114

going through with it. But you do not have to end the marriage.

4. If You Have Sinned by Getting an Unscriptural Divorce, Make Things Right

First, confess that you have sinned; then accept His forgiveness for your sin. Do not spend the rest of your life feeling like a second-class citizen. Your sin is in the past, just as the sins of others are in their past. Acknowledge to others the pain and suffering of divorce. You may be uniquely positioned to help someone else avoid the mistakes and heartache you have experienced. Serve God faithfully for the rest of your life. Don't run and hide; get involved and go to work. Every member of your church is a forgiven sinner.

5. Understand That There Are Innocent Parties

The most innocent parties are the children. Almost without exception, children feel responsible when their parents get divorced. They blame themselves and feel rejected. Reach out to them and tell them that they are not at fault. Give them hope for their future.

There are also innocent spouses. Usually both parties in a broken marriage are at fault, but there are cases when one spouse does nothing wrong, yet the marriage ends anyway. We had a lady in our church some years ago who married a young man at Bible college who, though she did not know it, was a homosexual. She was not responsible for his sin or for the destruction of their marriage in any way. Do not judge people who have been divorced.

6. Respect the Fact That People Who Have Been Forgiven for an Unscriptural Divorce Are Just As Forgiven As Those Who Have Committed Any Other Sin

Divorce has terrible consequences for families and for our society. God is not in favor of it. But we should not be against divorced people. When God forgives someone, they are completely forgiven. The past is remembered no more (Heb. 8:12). Love, help and encourage those who have been divorced. Go out of your way to be a help to them.

8

Money Trouble, Part One

Looking at Money God's Way

"And he [Jesus] said unto them, Take heed, and beware of covetousness: for a man's life consisteth not in the abundance of the things which he possesseth."—Luke 12:15.

Money is one of the many resources God gives us to manage on His behalf. Another is our time; another is our talent. Those things make up our life—money is just what we get in exchange for our time. My purpose in teaching on money is not to help you get rich. Rather it is to help you do the best you can as a steward of all of the resources

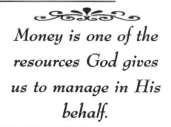

Money is one of the resources God gives us to manage in His behalf.

which God has entrusted to you, including your money.

Having a right spirit is more important than having what the world would call the right results. Peter preached the Gospel faithfully and saw three thousand souls saved. Stephen preached the Gospel faithfully and saw three thousand stones thrown at him! God was pleased with both men

117

because their hearts were committed to following Him.

It's important to realize that different people have different strengths and weaknesses when it comes to managing money. Because of their personalities and experiences, some will be more cautious, and some will be more willing to take greater risks. You need to identify both your strengths and your weaknesses in order to succeed at being a good steward.

I am not personally a great manager of details. That's not my strong point. There have been a few times in my life when I've been late paying a bill. It wasn't because we didn't have the money or didn't want to pay it. It was because I would forget to mail the payment. I have people at the church who help make sure those kinds of things are taken care of on time.

What I am good at is paying things off! We paid off the note on our church three years ahead of schedule. That saved us about $600,000. Another strength I have to some extent is the ability to see things that can be purchased and resold for a profit. I have been able to identify things that are good investments.

After you discover what your particular strengths and weaknesses are when it comes to money, wisdom says you should find people to help you shore up your weaknesses and find people you can help with your strengths.

The Bible has a great deal to say about money. It is filled with principles to help us be good stewards for the Lord. Those principles are being largely ignored today, including by believers. Surveys tell us that 70% of the people in the United States live from paycheck to paycheck. For them, this week's check pays this week's bills. Nothing is set aside for emergencies or future needs.

Less than 30% of the families in this country use a monthly budget to manage their money. The average

American spends a $1.22 for every dollar he earns! The personal savings rate in 2000 was 5.7%. By 2006, that had fallen to 3.6%. People are not being wise in the way they handle money.

Aside from their mortgage, the typical family in America has a debt of $38,000. (Some of you may be thinking that you're finally above average in something!) Ninety-five percent of the automobiles sold in this country are financed. The average car payment is $375 per month. Household debt as a percentage of disposable income exceeds 100%—most people owe more than they are worth.

We have money trouble in this country. Many people think that if they could just come into some money, if someone would leave them an inheritance or they could win the lottery (not a good idea), that would take care of their problems. William Post, who won $16 million in the Pennsylvania lottery in 1988, lives on Social Security. "I wish it had never happened," he told a reporter. "It was a nightmare."

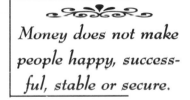

Money does not make people happy, successful, stable or secure.

A former girlfriend sued him for part of his money. His own brother hired a hit man to kill him so he could inherit the wealth. Other siblings hounded him to invest in their businesses. He spent time in jail for shooting at a bill collector. Within a year of winning the jackpot, he was a million dollars in debt, and he eventually declared bankruptcy.

Money does not make people happy, successful, stable or secure. Wise management of money according to the principles of the Word of God can do that.

The Provision

If we are going to manage our money wisely, we need to

understand some basic, foundational concepts about money. Everything you have was given to you by God. Over the years, I've had people say to me, "Everything I got, I got with these two hands." My reply is, "Where did you get your hands?"

We can never have the right attitude toward money until we have the right attitude toward God. We also need to understand His attitude toward our money. Finally, we need to see our responsibilities toward Him. If our thinking in these areas is correct, our money problems are well on their way to being solved.

> *Everything you have was given to you by God.*

1. God Is the Owner

"The silver is mine, and the gold is mine, saith the LORD of hosts."—Hag. 2:8.

"For this cause have I sent unto you Timotheus, who is my beloved son, and faithful in the Lord, who shall bring you into remembrance of my ways which be in Christ, as I teach every where in every church."—I Cor. 4:17.

"Every good gift and every perfect gift is from above, and cometh down from the Father of lights, with whom is no variableness, neither shadow of turning."—Jas. 1:17.

2. God Gives the Opportunity

"But thou shalt remember the LORD thy God: for it is he that giveth thee power to get wealth, that he may establish his covenant which he sware unto thy fathers, as it is this day."—Deut. 8:18.

"The blessing of the LORD, it maketh rich, and he addeth no sorrow with it."—Prov. 10:22.

3. God Sets the Obligation

"And all the tithe of the land, whether of the seed of the land, or of the fruit of the tree, is the LORD's: it is holy unto the LORD."—Lev. 27:30.

"Bring ye all the tithes into the storehouse, that there may be meat in mine house, and prove me now herewith, saith the LORD of hosts, if I will not open you the windows of heaven, and pour you out a blessing, that there shall not be room enough to receive it."—Mal. 3:10.

The Purpose

What is the purpose of money? To understand that, you have to understand what money is. Money is a medium of exchange. Take a look at a one-dollar bill. The value of the paper and ink is only a few pennies. But if you take it to the bank, they will give you a hundred pennies for it. That's because we have a cultural agreement that we will accept a piece of paper, basically worthless in and of itself, at "face value." Whatever the bill says on the front, we say it is worth that much money.

In the old days, before money came to be widely used, business was cumbersome. If one man raised sheep and another raised corn, it was difficult to make a trade. How many ears of corn does it take to equal a lamb? Who decides the value? It is much easier to carry a few coins to trade rather than a flock of sheep or bushels of corn.

In America, our paper money used to be backed by gold and silver. Before 1934, paper money was backed by gold. During the Great Depression, the government switched to silver. On each silver certificate (a one-dollar bill) printed between 1934 and 1963 it said: "This certifies that there has been deposited in the Treasury of the United States of America one silver dollar payable to the bearer on demand." In those days, you could take that dollar bill and trade it in for one dollar of silver bullion.

The politicians didn't like having the money tied to gold and silver, so they changed the rules. Now your dollar bill says: "This note is legal tender for all debts, public and private." You can't trade your dollar in for silver any more. Yet people still accept it as being worth one full dollar. Money is used by society for a medium of exchange. But what are God's designs for your money?

1. Money Is for Giving

"But seek ye first the kingdom of God, and his righteousness; and all these things shall be added unto you."—Matt. 6:33.

"He that giveth unto the poor shall not lack: but he that hideth his eyes shall have many a curse."—Prov. 28:27.

"Honour the LORD *with thy substance, and with the firstfruits of all thine increase:*

"So shall thy barns be filled with plenty, and thy presses shall burst out with new wine."—Prov. 3:9, 10.

The first thing anybody should do with the money God entrusts to them is to give. I'm glad that I learned to give before I learned to invest. I'm glad I learned to give before I learned to make money. I'm grateful that my parents taught me this principle when I was a boy.

> *The first thing that everyone should do with the money God has entrusted to them is give.*

A person who is not willing to give to the Lord is not obedient; and while he may have riches, he will never know God's blessing of contentment. You cannot be right with God and be wrong with your money. By giving to the Lord's work, we demonstrate our priorities and show where our love and allegiance lie.

2. Money Is for Living

"But if any provide not for his own, and specially for those of his own house, he hath denied the faith, and is worse than an infidel."—I Tim. 5:8.

I believe the Bible teaches us that the husband has the primary responsibility for meeting the financial needs of the family. At our church, we have a policy that we will not hire a woman for a full-time position if she has children under school age. I don't want to encourage them to work outside the home.

People sometimes ask me, "What if the wife needs to work so we can afford to live at a certain level?" I think if the wife earns money to help make the house payment or the car payment or to buy food, which is the husband's responsibility, he is asking her to help him do his job. So it only makes sense then that he help do her jobs—cooking, cleaning, child care and so forth.

It is wrong for a man to have his wife work all day so he can enjoy a better lifestyle and then expect her to do all of the housework while he props up his feet at the end of the day and asks her to cater to him. If she is helping him provide for the family, it is sinful and selfish for him not to reciprocate.

By the way, the government doesn't owe you anything. You are not owed a living wage, food stamps, welfare or anything else. Now I believe in helping the poor. But I think we ought to do it God's way. When the Bible talks about the poor, it is referring to people who are weak and feeble, those who are unable to work to provide for themselves. Those people deserve our help. People who *won't* work deserve nothing.

My grandfather reared seven children during the Depression. He would have died before he took money from the government. He worked hard all of his life to provide. You are supposed to pay your own way. Men are supposed to take care of their families.

When Dr. Curtis Hutson left the Forrest Hills Baptist Church to go into evangelism, he got a call from the pulpit committee. They said, "We have interviewed a man who is interested in the position, but he says he can't live on what we were paying you." Dr. Hutson replied, "He probably can't. I never could either. But I wanted to be putting into the church rather than taking out!" I like that attitude.

3. Money Is for Saving

"There is treasure to be desired and oil in the dwelling of the wise; but a foolish man spendeth it up."—Prov. 21:20.

"A good man leaveth an inheritance to his children's children: and the wealth of the sinner is laid up for the just."—Prov. 13:22.

When my wife's grandmother died, the bulk of her estate went to her three children. But there was also money left in her will for each of her grandchildren. One of the things we did with the money she left my wife was to buy a couch for our home. It was a special remembrance for us when we saw that couch, because it reminded us that her grandmother had saved to have something to leave behind.

If you are spending all that you make, you are not wise. Solomon said that it is the foolish people who spend it all. Many people who have struggled with discipline in saving benefit from having a payroll deduction savings plan. If your employer takes it out for you, you don't have to worry about saving money. Find a way to set aside some money for the future.

4. Money Is for Investing

"Then he which had received the one talent came and

*said, Lord, I knew thee that thou art an hard man, reaping
where thou hast not sown, and gathering where thou hast
not strawed:*

*"And I was afraid, and went and hid thy talent in the
earth: lo, there thou hast that is thine.*

*"His lord answered and said unto him, Thou wicked and
slothful servant, thou knewest that I reap where I sowed not,
and gather where I have not strawed:*

*"Thou oughtest therefore to have put my money to the
exchangers, and then at my coming I should have received
mine own with usury.*

*"Take therefore the talent from him, and give it unto him
which hath ten talents.*

*"For unto every one that hath shall be given, and he shall
have abundance: but from him that hath not shall be taken
away even that which he hath.*

*"And cast ye the unprofitable servant into outer darkness:
there shall be weeping and gnashing of teeth."*—Matt.
25:24-30.

It took me a long time to realize the importance of
investing. It's just not something that I heard much about
in church or in the Christian
school. It simply wasn't part of
my thinking that a Christian
should be an investor. Yet the
Bible does teach the importance of investing.

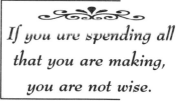

*If you are spending all
that you are making,
you are not wise.*

Notice the parable of the talents that Jesus told. The man
who received one talent was not a thief. He was not dishon-
est. He did not lose anything. He was not careless with
what had been entrusted to him. Yet because he did not
invest to earn a return, he was strongly condemned as
"wicked," "slothful" and "the unprofitable servant."

In most people's lives, there will come a few financial

windfalls. Maybe it's a few hundred dollars as an income tax refund. Perhaps someone dies and leaves you an inheritance. Or you could get a settlement from an accident or an injury. Over the years I have watched people in that situation. At that point, they have the choice either to spend the money or invest it in something that could pay off for the rest of their lives.

It is very difficult to get people not just to spend it. That is the natural human tendency. But if we do not invest, we are falling short of God's plan. The clear point of the parable of the talents is this: God expects us to take what He gives us and increase it. That is true spiritually, and that is the primary application of the parable Jesus taught. But this truth is also applicable to our finances. The Master always expects a return on His investment.

The Problem

We've already seen that many people, including many Christians, have trouble with money. I believe that most of those problems can be traced back to one of three wrong attitudes toward money.

1. We Worry

"Therefore take no thought, saying, What shall we eat? or, What shall we drink? or, Wherewithal shall we be clothed?

"(For after all these things do the Gentiles seek:) for your heavenly Father knoweth that ye have need of all these things.

"But seek ye first the kingdom of God, and his righteousness; and all these things shall be added unto you.

"Take therefore no thought for the morrow: for the morrow shall take thought for the things of itself. Sufficient unto the day is the evil thereof."—Matt. 6:31–34.

Worry makes us hoard.

"There is that scattereth, and yet increaseth; and there is that withholdeth more than is meet, but it tendeth to poverty."—Prov. 11:24.

Some people don't want to part with anything. They don't want to turn loose of any money, whether it is for the work of God or in the secular realm. They want to have their money where it is available to them.

Worry makes us self-centered.

"Look not every man on his own things, but every man also on the things of others."—Phil. 2:4.

We worry about things involving ourselves. I have never struggled to get to sleep at night wondering how my neighbor would pay his bills. But God is neither pleased nor honored when we are focused solely on ourselves.

Worry destroys faith.

"And immediately Jesus stretched forth his hand, and caught him, and said unto him, O thou of little faith, wherefore didst thou doubt?"—Matt. 14:31.

Worry and faith are opposites. Faith drives away worry; worry chases away faith. You cannot have both at the same time.

Worry keeps us from taking reasonable risks.

There are some things you can do to increase the resources God has trusted to you that require you to take a risk. You can always bury your money in the back yard, but we've already seen what God thinks of that approach. The fact that things could potentially go wrong should not be allowed to keep you from doing what you ought to do.

Any investment has some risk. In fact, all progress in any

area of life involves risk. The great scientist Louis Pasteur received many awards and accolades during his lifetime for his groundbreaking work. But when they asked him what he wanted inscribed on his tombstone, Pasteur asked for these words: "Joseph Meister lived."

Pasteur was studying immunization for various diseases. He had discovered that weakened forms of different viruses could offer protection against full-blown disease. When nine-year-old Joseph Meister was bitten by a rabid dog, his parents begged Pasteur to test his vaccine on the dying boy. Since Pasteur was not a doctor, he could have been prosecuted for practicing medicine without a license, but he took the risk and began a ten-day injection process that saved the boy's life. And when asked for words to sum up a lifetime of work, that was what Pasteur wanted to have remembered.

2. We Want

"He that loveth pleasure shall be a poor man: he that loveth wine and oil shall not be rich."—Prov. 21:17.

"He that loveth silver shall not be satisfied with silver; nor he that loveth abundance with increase: this is also vanity."—Eccl. 5:10.

People who live for fine things, those who want the latest and best and most expensive toys, will not accumulate wealth. Wanting things makes you too poor to get them. This is something of a paradox. You have to have control over your appetite for things before you can have enough to get things. If the things matter too much, you will spend yourself into poverty.

> *If "things" are too important to you, you will spend yourself into poverty.*

We live in a society that is given over to materialism. Each year billions of dollars are spent on advertising that is designed to create an appetite and desire for things in the hearts and minds of consumers. When we allow our desire for things to control us, we are replacing God. While we are far too sophisticated to bow down to a golden calf, Paul warns us that "covetousness...is idolatry." (Col. 3:5)

3. We Waste

"There is treasure to be desired and oil in the dwelling of the wise; but a foolish man spendeth it up."—Prov. 21:20.

Did you get an allowance when you were a child? I used to get a quarter a week when I was little. I remember that I couldn't wait to spend it. I had a quarter, and I could buy a candy bar. (I think I may be dating myself a little!) That's all I thought money was for—to buy things. We even have an expression for that attitude: The money is burning a hole in his pocket.

Over the years I have counseled so many people who were struggling with money problems. When we sit down to go over how they are spending what they have, I almost invariably find that they are simply wasting large amounts of their money. Frankly, that is the result of the same childish attitude I had toward my allowance—I've had it, and I wanted to spend it.

Rather than carefully planning and budgeting, most people spend on whim and impulse. As a result, they end up in debt. Someone once described Americans as "people who spend money they don't have to buy things they don't need to impress people they don't like." It is not true in every case, but most people who have money trouble are wasteful in their spending habits.

9

Money Trouble, Part Two

Fifteen Principles about Money

"So then every one of us shall give account of himself to God."—Rom. 14:12.

It is not how much you end up with, but what you do with what God has given you that will determine your rewards or lack of rewards at the judgment seat. There's no separate line for people who are rich. The parables of Jesus are filled with stories of a master calling on his servants to give an account of their work. One day you will answer to God for how you handled the resources He entrusted to you.

> *One day you will answer to God for how you handled the resources He entrusted to you.*

In the United States in 2005, there were around 4 million households with a net worth of a million dollars or more. On average, their annual taxable income was $131,000. Eighty percent of them are first-generation millionaires. They did not inherit that money from their parents or grandparents; they earned it.

These people share some interesting characteristics. Over half have lived in the same house for more than twenty years. Less than one quarter of them drive current-year cars. They are careful in how they spend and invest their money. God does not expect you to be a millionaire. That is not His will or plan for every person, and people who tell you it is are not being honest with the Bible. But He does expect you to be wise in how you handle your money.

A lot of Christians have a negative attitude toward money. They think it shows a lack of faith to save and invest. There was a time in my life when I thought there was something spiritual about "trusting God" instead of planning for the future. And it is important to have faith, but the Bible says a wise man saves for the future along with trusting God.

> *The use or misuse of money determines its moral value.*

The old farmers had a saying: "The best place to pray for corn is at the end of the hoe handle." While you are trusting God, establish a wise plan for your future. These fifteen principles will help you bring your thinking about money into line with God's, and, as a result, you will begin to enjoy His blessing on your finances.

1. None of it is yours—it all belongs to God.

"The silver is mine, and the gold is mine, saith the LORD of hosts."—Hag. 2:8.

A steward is a person who manages something that does not belong to him. All of your possessions ultimately belong to God. When we start to view our money as belonging to us, it changes our attitude toward it. We need to be careful to avoid what Jesus called "the deceitfulness of riches" (Matt. 13:22). When we realize God owns everything, it reminds us to be careful of how we take care of what He has entrusted to us.

2. Money is a neutral substance—it can be used for good or evil.

Money is neither good nor bad. It is the use or misuse of money that determines its moral value. The love of money is the problem, not the money itself (I Tim. 6:10). There is no connection between how much money you have and how spiritual you are. Neither riches nor poverty say anything about your standing with God. Neither is better than the other in and of itself.

3. Money can be invested forever, but it can be spent only once.

Dr. Bob Jones Sr. used to say, "Never sacrifice the permanent on the altar of the immediate." It is more fun to spend money, and it is not always wrong to spend money, but money, once it is spent, is gone forever. On the other hand, money that you invest will be working for you for years to come. It is important to keep your long-term priorities and goals in mind when you make your spending and investing decisions.

4. It is sinful to spend more than you have; it is foolish to spend all that you have.

"There is treasure to be desired and oil in the dwelling of the wise; but a foolish man spendeth it up."—Prov. 21:20.

When you buy something that you cannot afford, you are presuming on God and on the future. You should not buy things on credit cards and with installment loans that you will not be able to pay off just so you can have things now. And wisdom says that you should never spend all of the money that you make. You are not being spiritual because you avoid saving money. It is more important to give, but it is also God's plan for you to save some of your money.

5. Most financial problems can be traced to ignorance, indulgence or irresponsibility.

Sometimes people do not understand how to manage money. If no one has taught you proper money management, you have the responsibility to learn it. You cannot expect to prosper if you are focused on satisfying your appetites with your purchases. Some people have to have the latest car, TV, clothes or the biggest house. Those people are making foolish choices that will haunt them long into the future. You may have nice toys, but you will not have substance. By the way, there is no correlation between a person's desire to work and his desire to have.

> *If no one has ever taught you proper money management, it is your responsibility to learn it.*

6. God expects us to increase what He gives us.

"Thou oughtest therefore to have put my money to the exchangers, and then at my coming I should have received mine own with usury."—Matt. 25:27.

For years I knew this was true spiritually. I knew to take advantage of my opportunities in the spiritual realm to try to make the most of every one of them. But when I studied the Bible more thoroughly, I realized that the same principle holds in the financial world. God is looking for a return on His investment in us. We need to be wise in how we handle our money, recognizing that God expects us to be just as faithful and diligent with our money as we are with our talents and spiritual gifts.

7. God is against "get-rich-quick" schemes.

"He that hasteth to be rich hath an evil eye, and considereth not that poverty shall come upon him."—Prov. 28:22.

Many people are looking for a shortcut or an easy way to get rich. God is never behind such a scheme. I know several preachers who have suffered huge financial losses because they got on board with a financial scheme that they thought would be the answer to all of their financial needs. The plans, programs and systems you see on television are not the answer to your money problems. If those plans really worked, the people selling them would be using them for themselves rather than selling you a product.

8. God is against loving riches.

One of the things that makes money so tempting to people is that it can take the place of God in their hearts. That is why the Bible warns us against "the love of money" as "the root of all evil" (I Tim. 6:10). All kinds of evil actions and thoughts come from an unhealthy fixation on and devotion to money. And the love of money is not limited to rich people. Many poor people love money; they just don't have any.

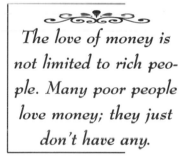

The love of money is not limited to rich people. Many poor people love money; they just don't have any.

9. God is against trusting riches.

If you are wise and save and invest your money, you have done the right thing. Yet that carries with it a danger—that you will come to trust in the money instead of in God. Paul instructed Timothy to warn the rich not to trust in "uncertain riches" (I Tim. 6:17). Money is no guarantee of security or happiness, and those who trust in it always end up disappointed.

10. God is not against riches.

Remember that God is not against your having money. Since His plan for funding His work in this world depends on the giving of His children, He is pleased when you have money—provided that the money does not really have you. The Bible is very clear that God gives us good things, including money, with the intention that we enjoy them (I Tim. 6:17). If God has blessed you with money, don't feel guilty about it; enjoy it and use it wisely.

11. The more you spend when you are young, the less you have to spend when you're old.

The willingness to defer the purchase of things until you can pay for them means that you will be better off financially. I do not think that it's wrong to have nice things. There's nothing spiritual about sitting on milk crates in a rented house. I like our couch. But we didn't start out with that couch when we first got married.

12. Spending should be deferred; giving should not.

Some people are waiting until they have it made before they start to give. The problem with that approach is that giving is primarily a spiritual decision rather than an economic one. On your scale of priorities, saving and investing should always come after giving. That is the attitude Jesus was describing in Matthew 6:33. Don't take God's money to put in your investment. And don't be reluctant to increase your giving if He puts that on your heart, even if it means you have less to save or invest.

13. Wealth and poverty are equally dangerous.

"Remove far from me vanity and lies: give me neither poverty nor riches; feed me with food convenient for me:

"Lest I be full, and deny thee, and say, Who is the LORD? or lest I be poor, and steal, and take the name of my God in vain."—Prov. 30:8, 9.

There is danger in both extreme wealth and extreme poverty. Either can damage our attitude toward God.

14. Money is not what life is about.

"And he said unto them, Take heed, and beware of covetousness: for a man's life consisteth not in the abundance of the things which he possesseth."—Luke 12:15.

Not long ago I went to preach for a special meeting in a small church. The pastor put me in a little motor lodge in the town. It wasn't the nicest place I've ever stayed, but the nearest big, chain motel was another thirty minutes away. That was the best place in town to stay. The pastor told me that he had invited another preacher a few months before who had refused to stay there! That man insisted on being put up in the big hotel thirty minutes away. The bed in that room wasn't much different from the ones in which I've slept in other places. I got a good night's sleep. There's nothing wrong with nice things, but money is not the meaning of life.

> *On your scale of priorities, saving and investing should always come after giving.*

15. You must pay for every purchase; wise people pay when they purchase.

So many offers today depend on making people think that they will not have to pay for what they buy. The zero-interest plans and deferred-payment options encourage you to buy things that you cannot afford by making you feel like you do not need to pay for them. Everything that you buy must be paid for eventually. It is far better for you to pay when you make the purchase rather than financing it and still be making payments long after the item is used up and gone.

10

Money Trouble, Part Three

A Plan for Getting Out of Debt

When my wife and I first got married, we didn't have many discussions about money. That's because we didn't have any money to decide how to spend. Everything we had went to the basics—tithe, food, housing, insurance and the things that are necessary to survive.

I remember the day we got our first credit card. I felt like a grownup. Now I didn't have to save up the money to get a new shirt and tie. I could get it all at once on the credit card and pay for it later. That credit card soon became a very good friend of mine...and then it became a very significant enemy.

Now we never went deeply into debt. My big credit card bill in those days totaled $500. But I was making $110 a week as an assistant pastor, so that represented more than a month's salary. Today the average household in America owes almost $10,000 on credit cards, not counting car loans, student loans or home loans. Total non-mortgage debt averages $38,000!

My beat-up old car barely ran. My father-in-law drove

it once, and he was appalled. He said, "I don't want my daughter riding in that car. Find out how much it will take to make the down payment on a decent car, and I'll loan it to you." He loaned us $500 that we put down on a $3,000 car, and we financed the rest. We paid him off in a year, but we still had the car loan. Now we had to pay that on top of the credit-card payment each month.

> *The number one cause for divorce in America is finances.*

Then I found a motorcycle. For just $24 a month, I could ride in style. So we added that to our budget as well. Before long, it was all I could do to make the payments each month. I had fallen into the typical "buy now, pay later" mentality that dominates American society.

After I had been a pastor for a couple of years, I made the commitment to the Lord and to my wife that we were going to get out of debt. Studies tell us that the number one cause for divorce in America is financial problems.

Principles to Understand

I'm going to share with you the principles that we followed to get out of debt. It was not an immediate release. It was a gradual process. There were times when I wasn't sure it was going to work. But in the end, these steps enabled us to pay off the credit cards and car loans and get out of debt. There are two things you need to keep in mind as we talk about getting out of debt.

1. Understand the Scripture

"The rich ruleth over the poor, and the borrower is servant to the lender."—Prov. 22:7.

The Word of God cautions us about being in debt,

because debt enslaves us. When every penny you earn is already promised to someone else, you are no better off than a slave, because nothing you have really belongs to you.

2. Understand the Psychology

Greed motivates us. We fall into the trap of thinking that we must have the newest item, the latest fashion, the newest model. We want to have the same toys that our friends and neighbors do. Greed is a consuming desire for material possessions. And that is the root of much of our financial instability.

Things master us. That new car is great when you first buy it, but after a few years you have to feed it. It needs a new exhaust system, new tires or a tune up. That which you bought to serve you is requiring additional spending—usually before you have even finished paying for it.

Debt murders us. People are absolutely suffocated by stifling mounds of debt they have piled on themselves. I

> *Debt will rob you of the joy and pleasure God means for you to experience.*

have counseled people who were so deeply in debt that they felt there was no hope they would ever get out. Debt will rob you of the joy and pleasure God means for you to experience.

Getting out of debt is much like trying to diet. I like being skinny (at least what I remember of it!)—the way my clothes fit, the fact that my knees didn't hurt and the extra energy I had. But I also like eating. I like candy bars. I like thick steaks and baked potatoes with butter and sour cream. I like French fries with cheese and barbeque sauce. I just like food! When I'm fat, I enjoy eating. When I'm skinny, I enjoy the benefits of being skinny.

The problem is that there is a long space between fat and skinny. And to make the trip, you have a period of time when you aren't enjoying eating because of the diet, but you can't enjoy being skinny because you aren't there yet. That is my least favorite time. But there is no way to get from where you are to where you want to be without going through that process of denial.

It's fun to buy things, even if you can't afford them. It's fun at the moment, but that pleasure doesn't begin to compare with the joy of being out of debt. To get out of debt, you have to go through a period when you aren't buying anything, but you don't have any money either. Still, it's worth it.

Those who buy things they don't need with money they don't have to impress people they don't like at least have the pleasure of consuming. They may dread going to the mailbox or answering the phone, but they at least had fun getting things. The person who is free from debt has the pleasure of paying bills when they're due without worrying about where the money will come from. He also avoids paying exorbitant interest on his purchases.

You will never get out of debt if you are not willing to go through the process of denial.

You will never get out of debt if you are not willing to go through the process of denial. There may be other effective means and plans; I am sharing with you what worked for us. But there are no plans that are instant and painless. Just as with dieting, you can't succeed by taking shortcuts. Commit yourself to this course of action, see what the benefits will be and maintain the course, even though at first all you have is the sense of denial.

I've used this plan with scores of couples over the years.

It's a lot of work to put it together, and it requires discipline to follow it. But I have never yet had a couple who put in the time and stuck to the plan for whom it did not work. I have had a few people who simply didn't have enough money even to get started. They had to alter their lifestyle drastically to cut expenses and bring in more income. Yet when they stuck to the process, they found that it worked. So here are some practical steps to help you get out of debt.

Actions to Take

1. Budget Allocation

Make a list of all monthly bills and regular expenses. Statistics say that less than thirty per cent of American families have a written spending plan. You need to know where your money is going before you can hope to begin getting out of debt. Now when most people sit down to make their list, they leave things out. If you pay your insurance every quarter or twice a year, it still must be included. You don't get a bill from the grocery store, but that is a regular, recurring expense for which you need to plan.

Have a miscellaneous category for smaller expenses. Things that are inexpensive do not necessarily need their own budget category. For example, a newspaper or magazine subscription should be in the miscellaneous category. Don't make the budget so complicated that you cannot keep up with it.

Divide each monthly obligation by the number of pay periods per month. If you get paid monthly, divide by one. If you get paid twice a month or every two weeks, divide by two. If you get paid every week, divide by four. Now if you get paid every week or every two weeks, that isn't quite the right math, but we're doing it this way on purpose.

Add up the total obligations per pay period and compare the sum to your take-home pay. Many times when I get people to this point, the ones I am counselling are in complete shock. Perhaps for the first time, they see why they've been having trouble making ends meet.

Make necessary adjustments. If your income does not equal your obligations, you are going to have to decrease spending, increase your income, or both. There are people who have to get an extra job or work overtime to make ends meet. But there are also many things on which people spend money which are not necessities. Cable television and Internet access are not essential to life. Eating out is not a necessity. Having two cars is something people lived without for years. Just because everyone else has it doesn't mean that you can't live without it.

Begin a budget notebook, either on paper or on the computer. There are plenty of sophisticated ways to budget, but I've found that the simple solutions are usually best. Make deposits into each account every time you get paid. Whatever amount you have allocated for your mortgage, car payment, credit-card payments and so forth should be credited to that item in the budget. Keep this record just like the register in your checkbook.

Set up a surplus account. If your budget is done properly, there should be at least a little left over each time you get paid. Even if it is only ten or twenty dollars, record that amount in the surplus category.

Record your expenses every time you spend the money. Write down the expenditure against the money that you have already credited to that account and "withdraw" it from the account when you write the check.

Spend only the extra money in your surplus or miscellaneous account for things that are not in your budget. Just having money in your bank account does not mean you can spend it—it may be committed to payments that are coming up. The only money that is free for spending is whatever is in the surplus account. You only have what is not owed.

2. Debt Reduction

Stop borrowing for depreciating items. Credit cards can be a useful tool. I have a credit card that I use. Most months, the bill totals between $5,000 and $10,000. But we pay it off in full every month. That total includes airline tickets for when I travel and speak, things that the church needs to purchase and other expenses related to the ministry. I am reimbursed for most of those things, and I always pay the bill in full so that I am not incurring interest charges.

I counsel couples to enforce discipline this way. The first time you have a month in which you do not pay the credit-card bill in full, put the credit card in a drawer. Do not take it out again until the bill is paid off. The second time that happens, take a pair of scissors and cut the card into little pieces. It doesn't make any sense to try to empty out a sink with a cup unless you first turn off the water. The first step to debt reduction is to stop adding additional debt.

> *It is God's money and not ours that we are wasting in the accumulation of things that are temporary.*

The average American adult receives seven credit card solicitations each year. (I think I get seven each month!) There is an enormous industry dedicated to getting you to use credit cards foolishly.

Be aware of the quarterly windfall. If you get paid weekly, you will have an extra paycheck four times a year. (If you get paid every two weeks, it will happen twice a year.) Your grocery, gas, giving and a few other accounts will not change. That money will need to be spent just as usual. But your monthly mortgage, car payments and credit-card payments are already covered by the other paychecks.

Pick one bill on which to pay extra. Take the money that is available from those monthly categories and put it together to make an extra payment on the smallest bill you owe or the one that is scheduled to be paid off the quickest. We started with the motorcycle payment. Since that was just $24 per month, it wasn't too hard to make an extra payment on that bill each month. By doing that, we paid the total off in less than half the time the loan was originally set to run.

When that bill is paid off, add the amount you have been paying on it to another bill. We added the $48 we had been paying on the motorcycle to our regular payment for the next bill. As I recall, that payment was around $70. So we were then paying $118 each month on that account. We continued that same process until we had paid off all of the debt we had accumulated.

The advantage of this method is that it is almost pain-free. In my case, it required us to come up with an additional $24 per month to get started. Then we just continued using the money we had been spending to pay down the total until we were done. This process escalates. Before long, you can see how it is working, and that will encourage you to stick to the plan. If you continue this process, you will be amazed at how quickly you start to get ahead.

3. Staying Out of Debt

Learn to purchase wisely. The biggest and most important purchase most people will ever make is their home, yet many people buy a house with very little thought for the future. (I'll talk more about principles for buying a house in the next chapter.) Don't spend money carelessly.

Buy things that you need according to your budget plan rather than spending on impulse.

Pay cash. The average American spends $1.22 for every $1.00 he earns. If you do not have the money to pay for something, wait. If you do use your credit card to purchase something, deduct that amount from your checking account balance then, rather than waiting until you actually write the check to pay the bill. That way you will be able to pay the bill in full when it comes due. Remember that the purpose of a credit card is not to allow you to buy things you can't pay for right away

Wait for nonessential items to go on sale. I recently bought a $450 suit on sale for $150. Now it is possible to buy a $150 suit for $150 pretty much any day of the week, but that is not a good purchase. The $450 suit looks better, is made better and will last longer. I did not have to buy a suit right away, so I waited until I found an excellent bargain that would give me the most value for my money.

Check the Internet. I am not an Internet expert. I don't spend much of my time surfing the web. But I do know that there are some tremendous deals out there. By investing a little time, you will often be able to find something much cheaper than you could find it locally.

Don't let your car drive you into the ground. Other than credit-card spending, people waste and lose more money on cars than on anything else. As the price of cars has gone up, the length of car loans has grown as well. Once it was rare to see a car loan that was longer than three years. Now it is not at all uncommon for car loans to run seven or even eight years! And the average car-loan payment is $375.

At this point in my life, I could afford to buy a brand new car. I could make the payments each month without struggling to come up with the money. I am currently driving a nine-year-old Lincoln Town Car. It's a beautiful car that rides well. It's in excellent condition. I got it at an estate sale for just over $5,900 when it had 41,000 miles on it. New, the car cost nearly $50,000. So for about 12 percent of the original cost, I got roughly two-thirds of the useful life of the car.

If you currently have debt on a car, keep the car until the debt is paid off rather than trading it in and adding on more debt. When it is paid for, try to drive it at least one year longer. During this year, continue to make the car payment, this time to yourself by putting it into a savings account. That will greatly increase the amount you have to put down on your next car.

Take as short a loan as you possibly can when you purchase the next car. The monthly payments on a shorter loan are higher, but because you will have your old car for a trade-in and one year's worth of payments saved up, your payments should not be a burden. Repeat this process once or twice, and you will be able to drive out of the dealership—the used car dealership—without a payment book.

Be unattached to things. All of us struggle with materialism. I read one author recently who stated that consumerism and its attending debt are to our generation what slavery was to Christians of the eighteenth and nineteenth centuries. It is an obvious sin except to those who practice it. Remember that it is God's money and not ours that we are wasting in the pursuit and accumulation of things that are only temporal.

> *Only eight per cent of Bible-believing Christians tithe regularly.*

Only eight per cent of Bible-believing Christians tithe regularly. The average Christian gives three per cent or less of his income to God. That is a commentary on our values and priorities. It is also largely a by-product of our thing-centered thinking.

Stewardship Evaluation

The following characteristics will allow you to evaluate how you are currently doing as a steward of the resources God has trusted to you. Look at your own life in light of these five stewards and see which one most closely matches where you are right now. Remember that if your evaluation does not come out the way you want it to, you can use the information about managing money that I've shared with you to change your situation.

Smart Steward

1. Pays all his bills on time
2. Has no consumer debt
3. Has one to two month's income in the bank as a cushion
4. Is investing for the future beyond Social Security or pension
5. Gives generously

Steady Steward

1. Pays all his bills on time
2. Has little or no consumer debt with the exception of a car loan
3. Has one to four week's income in the bank as a cushion
4. Has only Social Security or a pension for retirement
5. Gives faithfully (tithes and an occasional offering)

Shaky Steward

1. Pays most of his bills on time, but is late on one or more each month

2. Has consumer debt excluding car totaling 10–15% of take-home pay

3. Has no cushion for emergencies

4. Has only Social Security or a pension for retirement

5. Gives sporadically and robs God frequently (tithes occasionally)

Sinking Steward

1. Is late on one-third or more of his bills each month

2. Consumer debt excluding car totals fiteen per cent or more of take-home pay

3. Has no cushion for emergencies and charges gas and food on a credit card

4. Has only Social Security or a pension for retirement and may have borrowed against his pension

5. Seldom if ever gives and robs God regularly

Sunken Steward

1. Has items that are being repossessed

2. Is facing reorganization or bankruptcy

3. Is a reproach and a bad testimony as a Christian

4. Experiences remorse over his situation which can lead to

   a. Repentance, repaying, rebuilding and rejoicing; or

   b. Relief by buying something else he cannot afford, repetition in continuing his spending habits, and ruin

11

Money Trouble, Part Four

Principles for Increasing Assets

I have been going to church all of my life. I've heard thousands of sermons by hundreds of different preachers. I've read many commentaries and books about the Bible. Very, very rarely have I ever heard anyone address the subject of investing and increasing assets from a biblical standpoint. But I want to show you what God has to say about not just managing, but increasing your assets.

God Expects Us to Plan

Some years ago, I realized that my ministerial income will not be covered by the Social Security system. That means that when I reach an age when I cannot preach regularly anymore, there will be nothing, humanly speaking, on which I can live. If I had my way, I would preach till I die.

George Whitefield, the powerful evangelist, traveled back and forth between England and America preaching the Gospel and spreading revival. He preached to crowds consisting of tens of thousands of people and had a very effective ministry. During his seventh and final trip to

America when he was preaching in Massachusetts, some people came to the house where he was staying one evening and asked him to speak to them for a little while from the Bible. Whitefield lit a candle and told them he would "preach till the candle burned out." When the message was done, Whitefield went to bed and died in his sleep. I'd like to die that way—but I cannot presume on God to know that's what will happen.

I had been reading about real estate investing and talking to people who knew how that business worked. I told one of my pastor friends about my situation. At that point, we had basically zero net worth. We didn't owe anything, but we didn't own anything either! My friend encouraged me to make wise plans for the future to fulfill the obligation I have to provide for my family and leave something for my children and future grandchildren.

> *There is no substitute in God's economy for good, old-fashioned hard work.*

Everyone reading this is getting older. None of us are going to get younger. The only way to stop getting older is to die. Your future will be greatly shaped by the plans you make in the present.

Now I believe in faith. I trust God. I know He loves me, and I know that He has my best interests at heart. The Bible promises that He will repay those who give to His work. But none of that absolves me of my responsibility to plan.

The virtuous woman in Proverbs 31 was not an average housewife. Her husband was wealthy, and she was managing a large household. She had a number of servants to help her fulfill the responsibilities of maintaining the house. There was a lot on her plate. She could not succeed in her work if she was disorganized or haphazard in her approach. Someone once said, "To fail to plan is to plan to fail."

This woman was focused on the future. In the description we are given of her life, I believe we find seven crucial elements that made her successful in managing her finances.

1. Diligence

"She seeketh wool, and flax, and worketh willingly with her hands.

"She is like the merchants' ships; she bringeth her food from afar.

"She riseth also while it is yet night, and giveth meat to her household, and a portion to her maidens."

"She looketh well to the ways of her household, and eateth not the bread of idleness."—Prov. 31:13–15, 27.

There is no substitute in God's economy for good, old-fashioned hard work. Thomas Edison said, "Genius is 1 percent inspiration and 99 percent perspiration." Because she had so much to do and so many responsibilities, this lady worked. She got up early and was diligent in all the tasks. Even though she had servants to help, she worked with her own hands as well. She did not sit back and expect others to take care of her.

2. Investment

"She considereth a field, and buyeth it: with the fruit of her hands she planteth a vineyard."—Prov. 31:16.

She took the money that she had earned through working with her hands and bought a piece of land. She could have bought herself a new wardrobe. She could have purchased the latest HM (that's Hebrew Motors) chariot with all the bells and whistles.

Instead, after careful consideration, she bought a field that would be suitable for use as a vineyard. She bought plants to fill the fields. That is forward thinking. Typically, it takes three years before grapevines produce enough grapes to be commercially useful. Investing requires patience. She used the money she had made to do something that would make even more money in the future.

3. Discernment

"She perceiveth that her merchandise is good: her candle goeth not out by night."—Prov. 31:18.

She knew the value of the things she had made. She could not be talked into letting things go for less than their value. She also made sure that the quality of the things she made was topnotch. She was willing to stay up late to make sure that things were being done properly and that she knew what was going on.

Before you ever make an investment, you need to spend the time to become educated about that field. Otherwise, you are probably going to lose your money. Someone said, "There's a difference between education and experience. You get an education when you read the fine print; you get experience when you don't!"

4. Generosity

"She stretcheth out her hand to the poor; yea, she reacheth forth her hands to the needy."—Prov. 31:20.

This is really an interesting expression. In Bible times, when people begged, they reached out toward people walking by and asked for money. Rather than waiting for people to reach out to her, she reached out to them. She was looking for opportunities to be generous.

In your money management plan, you need to include generosity. The purpose of investing is not solely to pile up money. Successful investing increases your resources and your ability to meet the needs of the work of the Lord and the needs of others. The root of all sin is selfishness (II Tim. 3:2). Planning to give to others helps ensure that our money and investments will not gain control of our hearts and minds.

5. Quality

"She is not afraid of the snow for her household: for all her household are clothed with scarlet.

"She maketh herself coverings of tapestry; her clothing is silk and purple."—Prov. 31:21, 22.

This woman was not looking for cheap solutions. I tell people that if you have $200 to spend on a suit, it's better to wait until a $400 suit goes on sale than it is to buy two $100 suits. The most expensive isn't always the best, but there is a definite difference in quality that is worth an extra cost.

There is a tendency to cut corners in an attempt to save money. Don't buy junk. If you are investing in stocks, buy a company that is worth owning. If you are looking at land, buy a piece of land that will be worth something. Someone said, "The bitterness of poor quality lingers long after the sweetness of low price is forgotten."

6. Wisdom

"She openeth her mouth with wisdom; and in her tongue is the law of kindness."—Prov. 31:26.

Wisdom is more than knowledge. Wisdom is the proper application of knowledge. Seeing things from a godly perspective helps you make the right decisions when you face choices in your life—decisions that not only impress and please people, but decisions that please God.

Any successful plan for the future requires wisdom. There are dangers and risks involved in every investment.

Wisdom helps you avoid pitfalls and helps you recover from reversals or setbacks. If you are depending on your own wisdom rather than God's, your money management plan is not going to succeed.

7. Kindness

"She openeth her mouth with wisdom; and in her tongue is the law of kindness."—Prov. 31:26.

We do not associate kindness with business success. When I asked people in my church to name a famous businesswoman, the most common response was Martha Stewart. She is good at a lot of things, but she is not known for being nice.

When I asked them to name a businessman, they named Donald Trump. I've never watched *The Apprentice,* but "you're fired" has become a buzzword. Success does not require meanness. You can always be nice, even when you are holding your ground and taking a stand. Kindness governed the words of the Proverbs 31 woman.

God Expects Us to Produce

"For even when we were with you, this we commanded you, that if any would not work, neither should he eat.

"For we hear that there are some which walk among you disorderly, working not at all, but are busybodies.

"Now them that are such we command and exhort by our Lord Jesus Christ, that with quietness they work, and eat their own bread."—II Thess. 3:10–12.

God's plan is for us to help those who cannot help themselves. We are supposed to care for the aged, the sick, the widows and orphans. There is no plan in the Bible for feeding people who could work but won't. The purpose of a financial plan is not so that you get to sit around and loaf all day. Rather, working is a vital and integral part of any Bible-based money management system.

1. God Commends Labor

"In all labour there is profit: but the talk of the lips tendeth only to penury."—Prov. 14:23.

I've talked to people who were in the army who were ordered to take a stack of bricks one at a time and move them to the other side of the drill area. After they were finally done, they would be ordered to reverse the process and move them back to where they were in the first place. Why would they do that?

The drill instructors are teaching discipline, obedience to orders and hard work. Those are qualities that every soldier (and every Christian) needs to be suc-

> *Working is a vital and integral part of any Bible-based money management system.*

cessful. Hard work is always valuable. My daughter Katie is taking a Bible doctrines class in our Christian school. I was helping her go over one of her assignments and saw that they were studying Sabellianism. Now that's an in-depth Bible class for high school! (Sabellianism is an ancient heresy regarding the relationship between the members of the Trinity.)

My wife said, "Honey, why are they studying that?" I said, "Because the teacher hates them!" No, that's not it at all. Almost all false doctrine can be traced back to errors in the early church. And the more we understand about those errors, the better protected we are from false doctrine. I'm glad Katie has some tough teachers. It's good for her to work hard and learn as much as she can.

2. God Condemns Laziness

"The soul of the sluggard desireth, and hath nothing: but the soul of the diligent shall be made fat."—Prov. 13:4.

Lazy people want the same things hard-working people want. Their ability to covet, desire and wish for things is not hindered by their slothfulness.

"I went by the field of the slothful, and by the vineyard of the man void of understanding;

"And, lo, it was all grown over with thorns, and nettles had covered the face thereof, and the stone wall thereof was broken down.

"Then I saw, and considered it well: I looked upon it, and received instruction.

"Yet a little sleep, a little slumber, a little folding of the hands to sleep:

"So shall thy poverty come as one that travelleth; and thy want as an armed man."—Prov. 24:30–34.

In his devotional *Morning and Evening* (November 24 evening), Charles Spurgeon wrote: "The worst of sluggards only asks for a *little* slumber; they would be indignant if they were accused of thorough idleness. A little folding of the hands to sleep is all they crave, and they have a crowd of reasons to show that this indulgence is a very proper one. Yet by these *littles* the day ebbs out, and the time for labour is all gone, and the field is grown over with thorns.

"It is by *little* procrastinations that men ruin their souls. They have no intention to delay for years—a few months will bring the more convenient season. Tomorrow, if you will, they will attend to serious things; but the present hour is so occupied and altogether so unsuitable, that they beg to be excused. Like sands from an hourglass, time passes, life is wasted by driblets, and seasons of grace are lost by *little* slumbers."

God Expects Us to Profit

When I was a young pastor, I would say, "I would rather give my money away than save it, because God pays better interest than the Second National Bank." That is true. I am grateful that my parents taught me about tithing and giving. I'm glad that God has enabled me to increase my giving over the years, so that each year I have the privilege of giving Him more than the year before. Giving is more important than saving and investing. But that does not mean that saving and investing should be ignored.

In Matthew 25, we see the parable Jesus told about the servants and the talents. Each man was given a different number of talents, depending on his ability. The man who was given five talents gained five more talents, and the man who was given two talents gained two more talents. Even though there was an absolute difference in their return, the rate of return was the same, and each received the same commendation from the master.

But the servant who was given one talent received a harsh condemnation. He hid his talent so that he would not lose it, but he gained nothing. He did not steal or waste his master's money. He did not make worthless investments. He did not frivolously spend it. He kept everything that he had been given by his master. He even wrapped the talent to keep it from being damaged by its burial in the ground.

The servants were not charged with just keeping what they had been given. If that is all the master had wanted, he could have taken the money with him. Their charge was to produce something in his absence with that which they had been given so that when he returned, he would have more than he did when he left.

"His lord answered and said unto him, Thou wicked and slothful servant, thou knewest that I reap where I sowed not,

159

and gather where I have not strawed:

"Thou oughtest therefore to have put my money to the exchangers, and then at my coming I should have received mine own with usury.

"Take therefore the talent from him, and give it unto him which hath ten talents.

"For unto every one that hath shall be given, and he shall have abundance: but from him that hath not shall be taken away even that which he hath."—Matthew 25:26–29.

Wise investors put their money where it makes money. That is what God does. When we demonstrate that we are faithful with what He has already given to us, He gives us more to produce an even greater result. This is true in both the physical and the spiritual realms.

Practical Strategies

These strategies are, by and large, not drawn directly from Scripture. However they have been used and have proven to be wise over the years. Many of them require an adjustment in the way you think about and handle money. But I have been counseling people for many years, and those who have followed these steps have found them to be very helpful.

1. Save a Cushion for Emergencies

It is wise to have one to three month's of your salary laid aside. If you do not have something in reserve when things go wrong, it will derail you. I know some people who buy groceries with a credit card. Paying 18 or 24 or even 32 per cent interest on milk and bread is a one-way ticket to poverty. Some people use credit cards for purchases like this to get frequent flyer miles or reward points, and as long as you pay off the entire balance every month and do not pay any interest, that can work. However, for most people, using a credit card for normal expenses of life is a result of not having any reserve in place.

Sometimes when I counsel people about saving money, they say, "But when I save money, I just turn around and spend it." To that I reply, "Don't!" That is not what that money you save is meant to accomplish. It is for a specific purpose—emergencies—and it should only be used for that purpose. When you do not have a cushion, you make bad judgments.

2. Invest in a Retirement Account

Look at what is available to you. Some people have 401(k) accounts where they work. Some teachers and preachers are eligible for a TSA (tax-sheltered annuity) that has certain advantages. Most people can also contribute to an IRA (individual retirement account). The

> *Using the credit card to purchase daily necessities is a one-way ticket to poverty.*

advantage of these accounts is that you do not pay taxes on the money until you retire.

A few years ago, they added a different kind of retirement savings plan called a Roth IRA. In this plan, you pay the taxes up front, but then when you take the money out, you do not pay taxes, regardless of how much the account increases. Whichever plan is best for you (and you should find a trusted financial advisor to help you make the decision), start investing in your retirement right now.

3. Purchase a Home That Is an Investment

The primary purpose of your home is for you to live in it and enjoy it. I counsel people to buy the nicest home they can reasonably afford. Your home is the only investment that can increase in value every day at the same time that it is being used every day. There are also, thanks to recent changes in the law, great tax advantages to owning a house, especially if you make money when you sell it.

For example, I encourage people to buy a home in a better neighborhood, even if they could buy a little more house for the money in a worse neighborhood. When the time comes to resell, the neighborhood will be as much or more of a determining factor in valuing the house as anything else. Purchase your home for comfort and the needs of your family, for use for the cause of Christ, but also for its investment potential.

Consider the likely appreciation. After we had lived in a house for about seven years, a realtor came and asked if we would be willing to sell it. We did not have the house on the market, but when he told me what they would pay for it, I got interested in selling. We had made some improvements and added on to the house, and they were willing to pay almost double what we had originally paid.

When we decided to sell the house, we started looking for a new place to live. I took into account the future value of houses in different neighborhoods. The choice for us came down to Frankenmuth or Birch Run. I could not afford what I wanted in Frankenmuth, so we bought some land and built a house in Birch Run. Appreciation was not the only consideration (my first consideration was the location in relation to the church), but it should be high on your list.

Consider the possible improvements. Are there things in the house that you can do to improve its value in the future? Now you need to be careful in this area, because some improvements add more value to the house than others. Spending $40,000 on renovations does not necessarily mean that the value of your home will increase by an equal amount.

Do your research and find out which items will add the most value in the future. Some people have greatly increased the value of their house simply by painting it. Some floor plans lend themselves to putting in an addition later. On the other hand, people who pay to put in a swimming pool do not usually get their money back in increased value. If you have skills and ability to do home improvement projects yourself, you can add a tremendous amount of "sweat equity" to the value of your house.

Consider how the house compares to others in the same neighborhood. It is better to buy the worst house in a better neighborhood than the best house in the worst neighborhood. It is tempting to try to maximize the house you can buy for the amount of money you have available, but it will rarely prove to be a good long-term decision. Over time, neighborhoods tend to decline rather than improve. So starting in a neighborhood that is already on a downward trend is usually not the best choice.

Consider the housing trends. Take time to research with real estate agents, bankers or on the Internet to determine what is happening in the housing market in your area. Find out which parts of town are expected to be the most desirable in the future. Look at what style and size of houses people are building and buying. These factors will be a major factor in determining the future value of your house when the time comes to sell.

Consider your family's needs and desires. Your home is not primarily an investment. Its value in the future should be secondary to its use in the present. When we built our house, we wanted to have a great room. We might have done that differently if we had been more focused on resale. But we expected to live there for years, and so we built the house to suit our life.

4. Purchase a Second House

Do not sell your house when you outgrow it. This is the

simplest way I know to increase assets, but most people do not take advantage of it for their future. When you reach the point of needing a bigger house, consider refinancing it instead. Take the money that you have gained from the appreciation and buy another house. Then you can rent out the first house and have someone else make the payments for you.

Doing this successfully requires an investment of time on your part to learn what you are doing. Real estate is a great investment, but it is far from risk-free. Talk to people who have done it. Talk to reliable real estate agents. Understand when you begin that there will be problems as well. Tenants will not be as careful as you were when you lived there.

By doing this, without taking any further money out of your pocket, you are building equity in two homes instead of one. It will require you to be willing to put up with the grief of being a landlord. If you are willing to do this, you will gain significant tax advantages (depreciation, an interest deduction and so forth), and you will build your net worth.

Not everyone has the mindset or the willingness to take the risks that are required for real estate investing. But there are a number of options for acquiring real estate that will produce an ongoing stream of income. Besides purchasing other properties to rent out, you could purchase properties to fix up and sell. You might also purchase properties to sell on a "land contract" or rent-to-own basis.

Again, do not take any of these steps without spending time (a lot of time) learning the market in your area. Some people have nearly ruined themselves buying land or properties that they should never have purchased. There are many opportunities in this area, but also many dangers.

Many people misquote what the Bible says about getting advice. People often say, "In a multitude of counselors is wisdom." But Solomon wrote, "Where no counsel is, the people fall: but in the multitude of counsellors there is *safety*" (Prov. 11:14, emphasis added). Seek wise counsel before you make any investment decision.

There are many things you can do to increase your assets. I happen to know more about real estate than some of the others. Find something that you can do to increase the resources with which God has prospered you. Ask God for wisdom (Jas. 1:5) as to how you can increase your assets.

At the end of my life, I want to be a blessing rather than a burden. I do not want my children to try to figure out how to pay for medical care I may need. I want to be able to help them even when I'm older. I want to leave an inheritance to my grandkids some day. The Bible says that is what a good man does (Prov. 13:22). So while I am giving to the Lord's work, I am also working to increase my assets for the future. My desire is to be a wise servant who is commended rather than a wicked and lazy one who is condemned.

12

When You Lose Your Leader

"And the people served the LORD all the days of Joshua, and all the days of the elders that outlived Joshua, who had seen all the great works of the LORD, that he did for Israel.

"And Joshua, the son of Nun, the servant of the LORD, died, being an hundred and ten years old.

"And they buried him in the border of his inheritance in Timnath-heres, in the mount of Ephraim, on the north side of the hill Gaash.

"And also all that generation were gathered unto their fathers: and there arose another generation after them, which knew not the LORD, nor yet the works which he had done for Israel.

"And the children of Israel did evil in the sight of the LORD, and served Baalim:

"And they forsook the LORD God of their fathers, which brought them out of the land of Egypt, and followed other gods, of the gods of the people that were round about them, and bowed themselves unto them, and provoked the LORD to anger."—Judg. 2:7–12.

This passage is a powerful illustration of what can happen when the people of God lose their leader. Moses was followed by Joshua. During Joshua's lifetime, the people continued to follow God. And although Joshua did not have a designated successor, the elders who served with him kept the people on track. But when that generation was gone, the people turned away from God and began worshiping idols.

Leadership is good. It is established by God. Sociologists have something they call the Iron Law of Oligarchy. That simply states that in any group of two or more, someone will be the leader. Dr. Lee Roberson was famous for saying, "Everything rises and falls on leadership." Good spiritual leaders are a tremendous blessing. They help us grow in our spiritual walk and point us to Christ.

> *Everything rises and falls on leadership.*

But your relationship with your leader is not your ultimate relationship as a child of God. It is not the end; it is merely a step toward the end, which is your personal relationship with God Himself. You cannot become a strong Christian on the back of someone else's walk with God. Because of an improper view of our relationship with our leaders, many of us falter when we lose a leader, either through death or disqualification from the ministry.

The Pattern

1. The Spiritual Leader

There is someone who has the hand of God on his life. He preaches the Word with power. He dedicates his life to teaching people to do what is right and encouraging them to love and serve God.

2. The Sincere Followers

These people recognize that the spiritual leader is teaching them according to the Scriptures. They see that following him is drawing them closer to God. They grow to appreciate, admire and love him. (There is nothing wrong with that.)

3. The Strong Influence

I believe the greatest graduates of Bob Jones University came during the time when Dr. Bob Jones Sr. was in charge. That was not the school's greatest day academically. That was not when they had their best facilities. But they had a strong leader. First-generation leaders tend to have a raw faith and vision that transfer to the next generation.

A person who is carving out territory and claiming it for Christ is forced to have a personal walk with God that develops a strength greater than that which is required to maintain a ministry. Please understand that I am grateful for second-generation leaders. It would be a tragedy if no work for God continued past the life of its founder. However, you will never get the same depth of faith that you get from the first generation from those who come after them and continue their work.

4. The Sudden Change

Perhaps the leader dies, relocates or even does something that removes him from his position. We see this in the life of King Joash (II Chron. 24). As long as Jehoiada the priest was alive, Joash followed God. But when Jehoiada died, Joash listened to evil counselors who drew his heart away from God. Joash lost the spiritual leader to whom he had become attached.

The Problem

1. Knowing About God Rather Than Knowing Him

169

Followers can become so attached to the leader that they substitute his relationship and walk with God for their own. So rather than truly knowing God, they know *about* God. They believed in God because the leader talked about what God had done in his life. They heard about the demonstration of God's power. They know what the leader told them about God, but they do not have a deep personal knowledge and relationship with Him.

> *Followers can become so attached to the leader that they substitute his relationship and walk with God for their own.*

I knew about Dr. John R. Rice. I heard him preach a few times. I almost got close enough to shake his hand once at a preacher's luncheon in 1977. I read his books—but I did not know him. I knew Dr. Curtis Hutson. I spent hours with him, listening to him talk about various topics and asking him questions. That was a relationship on an entirely different level.

2. Hearing About God's Works Instead of Seeing Them

In the Sunday night services at our church, we have something we call "The Hand of God." We have people give testimonies of what God is doing in their lives right now. One of the reasons for that is that we want our young people to see what God is doing today rather than just hear about what used to happen.

You need some of your own stories to tell. You need to see God at work in your life. You need to have answered prayers and truths from Scripture that you have found for yourself. My father took me with him often when he went soul winning. Watching people pray to accept Christ as Saviour made me believe that it was possible! No one had to convince me that God could save people—I saw it happen time and time again.

3. Standing on the Leader Instead of Standing on the Lord

Years ago a pastor in a town close to where I was pastor went through a couple of church splits and was having a hard time. He was a good man, and he was trying to get the people to do right, but some of them did not want to go along. He would sometimes call me for advice, and I tried to help him.

One night they had a vote that went against him. One of his friends asked him what he was going to do. The pastor replied, "I don't know. I haven't talked to Brother Ouellette yet." I believe in seeking counsel. It is wise and biblical to do so. But I am not the source of wisdom and direction. He needed to (and did) learn to seek God for himself rather than rely on me (or anyone else for that matter).

I believe in the priesthood of the believer. You are supposed to go to God directly for yourself. People are *helpful,* but only God is *necessary.* People can *advise* us, but only God can *direct* us infallibly. People who stand only on their leader will not know what to do when he is gone.

The Protection

1. Obligations of the Leader

The leader must attach his followers to God rather than to himself. It is unwise for the leader to focus too much attention on himself. I know one preacher who asked his assistant pastor, "Do you have the people going on my birthday celebration yet?" Another pastor called some people together and appointed them as a committee to take care of his gifts at Christmas and for his birthday and his anniversary.

The Bible does teach that a leader is worthy of honor. But as a leader, you need to let that take care of itself rather than trying to arrange things to call attention to yourself. Proverbs 27:2 says, "Let another man praise thee, and not thine own mouth; a stranger, and not thine own lips."

> *The main job of the leader is to get the people to love and follow God.*

The main job of the leader is not to get people to love and follow him; it is to get them to love and follow God. I tell the people at my church that if they love me more than they love God, I'm a bad leader. One day if the Lord does not return first, the First Baptist Church of Bridgeport will have to look for a new pastor. If the members of the church are depending on my spirituality instead of theirs, many of them will go away from God. I do not want that to happen.

The leader must talk about God more than himself. Personal illustrations are fine for a preacher to use. The apostle Paul used them when he preached. But their purpose should not be to get people to think, *Wow, what a great leader we have.* They should be intended, planned and presented so that people think, *Wow, what a great Lord we have.*

> *The first step that the leader takes away from God is the first step the follower must take away from the leader.*

The leader must teach commitment to principle rather than to places or people. Paul wrote, "Be ye followers of me, even as I also am of Christ" (I Cor. 11:1). Paul was not trying to get people to go blindly with him wherever he went; he was trying to get people to go with him after Christ. The first step the leader takes away from God is the first step the follower must take away from the leader.

It has been awkward for me sometimes to go a different direction than men who instructed, helped, influenced and encouraged me. But when they have wanted me to do things that I could not do and be true to the Bible, I have had to make that decision. Some years ago, a preacher was telling me about another pastor who thought for himself and made his own decisions based on the Word of God rather than on political influence. He said, "He's a maverick—kind of like you." I am not sure he meant that as a complete compliment, but I would rather be known as someone who stands alone for right than someone who goes along with what is popular.

2. Obligations of the Learner

The learner must know Christ for himself. A follower cannot tell whether the leader is following Christ unless he also knows Christ. You must read the Bible, pray and let the Spirit of God speak to your heart. Develop convictions for yourself rather than having them because they are the rules of the church.

The Christians at Berea were described as "more noble" because they went to the Word of God to determine if what Paul was teaching was correct (Acts 17:11). Too many church members accept anything that is said. I

> *A follower cannot tell whether the leader is following Christ unless he is following Christ himself.*

do not believe in being hypercritical or playing "gotcha" with the pastor, but error comes into the church when the Bible is not the standard against which all things are measured.

The learner must love the leader but worship God. One

173

follower of a great man of God was preaching. He said, "You ask, are you talking about the leader or Jesus? What difference does it make?" Frankly, it makes all the difference in the world! The greatest leaders you will ever know fall far short of His greatness and glory.

We follow men who have been placed over us by God only as long as they follow Him. When their authority contradicts that authority of Scripture, we have to stay with the Word of God rather than people.

Know the Book and know the God of the Book yourself. Someday your leader will be gone. If you have not developed a deep personal relationship with God, you will backslide.

13

Do You Need to Kill a Giant?

All through this book, we have looked at different challenges people face. If you live long enough, you are going to face most of these problems. The question is how we will respond when we face giants in our lives. Whether it is grief, temptation, money problems, issues with our children or dealing with the loss of a loved one, we will face a moment when we can either give up in defeat or, through faith, win a great victory for God. You can kill the giants that come against you.

I would have liked to have seen David fight Goliath. Of all the stories in the Bible, that is one of the two or three that stand out most vividly in my mind. I can see the Philistines camped on one hill and the Israelites across the valley camped on another hill. Neither army could move because of the landscape. Advancing toward the enemy would require you to march uphill into a rain of arrows and stones. So they stayed where they were.

I can hear the trumpets blowing as Goliath came out to shout his challenge to the people of God. Standing more than nine feet tall, he towered over everyone else. No one was willing to risk his life against the giant. Even King Saul, who was a full head taller than any of the other Israelites, refused to accept the challenge.

Knowing human nature, I imagine that each day the words of Goliath became a little harsher, and his insults, more biting. But no matter what he said, no one was willing to stand against him. Then one day David showed up. Three of his brothers were in the army, and Jesse sent his youngest son with a care package for them and to get a report on what was happening.

> *With God on our side no challenge is too difficult.*

Just as David arrived, Goliath came forth to issue his daily challenge. I think, although the Bible doesn't say so, that when David heard the Philistine's words, he expected Saul or one of the soldiers to do something about them. But no one did. They were all afraid. David heard the talk among the soldiers about what would be given to the man who defeated Goliath, and he thought that sounded pretty good.

So even though all of the trained men of war, their leaders and even the king were fearful, David walked down into the valley. There he picked up five stones, put one in his sling, killed the giant and won the battle. His faith in God carried him forward against a giant that no one else thought he could defeat.

Every one of us faces challenges and battles in life. We are not going to be, as the songwriter put it, "carried to the skies on flowery beds of ease." But the good news is that with God on our side, there is no challenge too difficult. No giant that we face is too strong to be defeated.

David Awakening to the Cause

David was not part of the army. He wasn't there to participate in the battle. He had none of the military equipment that men carried into battle in those days. He just came to bring some food to his brothers. But something happened in David's heart that turned him from a spectator to a soldier.

1. The Aggression of God's Enemy

When David saw that swaggering soldier from the Philistine army make his boasts and insult God's people and their God, he was indignant. David asked, "Who is this uncircumcised Philistine, that he should defy the armies of the living God?" (I Sam. 17:26). It is no secret that the world is the enemy of Bible Christianity. It's interesting to me that today you can't make fun of different races and cultures (and you shouldn't), but it's perfectly acceptable to make all kinds of jokes at the expense of Christians.

People are extremely careful to avoid giving offense to Muslims, but Christians are fair game. This world in which we live is against us. That has always been the case, and it will always be the case. Jesus said, "If the world hate you, ye know that it hated me before it hated you" (John 15:18).

2. The Apathy of God's People

The army of Israel was afraid of Goliath. They weren't willing to face him. Even though they had the true and living God on their side, their faith was weak. They preferred a stalemate with an enemy who mocked and ridiculed them and their God to the risk of a battle.

Many Christians today have settled for a truce with the world. In World War II, Vidkun Quisling, a Norwegian politician, encouraged people to cooperate with the Nazis. His name has become synonymous with giving in to the enemy instead of resisting. God does not want us to get along with the world; He wants us to fight. And the fact that many believers are not willing to do so does not mean that, in His power, we cannot both fight and win.

In fact, David basically said, "If nobody else wants to fight this guy, I will!" Dr. Bob Jones Sr. used to say, "You and God make a majority in any situation." Even if no one else is willing to stand up for what is right, you can. The fact that others are apathetic does not hinder you from defeating your giant.

3. The Award of God's Leader

The first thing David said was not, "Is there not a cause?" or "The battle is the LORD'S." The first thing David said was, "What shall be done to the man that killeth this Philistine, and taketh away the reproach from Israel?" (I Sam. 17:26). Some people are opposed to the idea of serving God for reward. But God put a reward system in place for serving Him.

God rewards us both on earth and in Heaven for doing right. David wanted to know what to expect. Marrying the king's daughter and having his family free from paying taxes forever sounded like a good deal to him. I do not believe that the rewards were David's primary motivation for fighting, but they did give him an extra incentive.

I want you to know that God takes good care of His people. He keeps a record of what we do for Him, and there is no chance that anything you do, even a cup of cold water, will be ignored or overlooked (Mark 9:41).

David Accepting the Cause

Because of what he had heard and seen, David determined to accept Goliath's challenge and meet him in battle. Now you might think that after forty days of listening to Goliath's bragging and being stuck in a stalemate with the enemy, the people would have been delighted that someone was willing to accept the challenge of the giant. But that is not what happened.

1. David's Motives Were Questioned

Eliab was David's oldest brother. According to the Scriptures, he was an impressive man. In fact, when Samuel saw Eliab, he immediately assumed that he was the man chosen by God to be the next king of Israel (I Sam. 16:6). But Eliab did not have the faith in God he needed to succeed. And he was jealous of David because he did have that faith.

"And Eliab his eldest brother heard when he spoke unto the men; and Eliab's anger was kindled against David, and he said, Why camest thou down hither? and with whom hast thou left those few sheep in the wilderness? I know thy pride, and the naughtiness of thine heart; for thou art come down that thou mightest see the battle."—I Sam. 17:28.

If you face the giants in your life, you are not going to get universal approval. Some people will be upset because they haven't been willing to do the same thing. The fact that you are willing to take on the challenge embarrasses them because they don't have enough faith. They would rather have the giant win than see you triumph over the enemy they cannot defeat.

2. David's Methods Were Criticized

The soldiers carried armor, shields and swords. Goliath had a massive spear. But all David had was a slingshot. No one thought that David would be able to fight effectively using that. Saul took his own armor and put it on David. (Remember that Saul was the tallest man in the kingdom.) It didn't fit, of course.

The methods and weapons of fighting that worked for Saul didn't work for David. He said, "I cannot go with these; for I have not proved them" and took the armor off (I

Sam. 17:39). By the way, if Saul's armor was so good, how come he didn't use it against Goliath? He wanted David to fight using equipment he was not willing to use himself.

David knew the slingshot worked. It wasn't fancy. It wasn't new. It wasn't impressive. But it worked. The basic tools of the Christian life—Bible reading, memorization, prayer and church attendance—work. There will always be someone willing to share a new way with you. Stick to the proven weapons of spiritual warfare. Keep on using what God has given you. Trust Him and go forward into battle.

3. David's Maturity Was Compared

Saul looked down on David because he was just a young man. He compared David's experience to Goliath's and found it wanting. If you are willing to enter into the battle against your giant, you may well find that people will say you aren't mature enough for the battle. But the truth is that people of every age face trials and giants. And if you don't fight them when you're young, it doesn't get easier when you're older; it gets harder.

Whether you've been saved for three weeks or thirty years, it is God who wins the battle. As David said, "The battle is the LORD'S" (I Sam. 17:47). Don't listen to people who tell you that you can't do anything because you're too young or inexperienced. There are always going to be people around who tell you that you can't; if you listen to them, you will never win the victory. Ignore them.

The poet Edgar Albert Guest wrote these words:

It Couldn't Be Done

Somebody said that it couldn't be done,
   But he with a chuckle replied
That "maybe it couldn't," but he would be one
   Who wouldn't say so till he tried.
So he buckled right in with the trace of a grin

On his face. If he worried, he hid it.
He started to sing as he tackled the thing
That couldn't be done, and he did it!

Somebody scoffed: "Oh, you'll never do that;
At least no one ever has done it."
But he took off his coat, and he took off his hat,
And the first thing we knew, he'd begun it.
With a lift of his chin and a bit of a grin,
Without any doubting or "quiddit,"
He started to sing as he tackled the thing
That couldn't be done, and he did it.

There are thousands to tell you it cannot be done;
There are thousands to prophesy failure.
There are thousands to point out to you one by one
The dangers that wait to assail you.
But just buckle in with a bit of a grin;
Just take off your coat and go to it.
Just start in to sing as you tackle the thing
That "cannot be done," and you'll do it.

David Advancing the Cause

We have the advantage of knowing how the story of David turns out. He didn't have that. What David had was faith in a God who was a whole lot bigger and stronger than the giant. You have that same God. And when you, in faith, go into battle, He is able and willing to give you the victory. Because David stood up to Goliath, the cause of Israel was advanced.

1. Concerned for the Testimony of the Army

He realized that every day that went by without Goliath's challenge being answered brought shame and reproach to the army of Israel. He recognized that they were being cowards by refusing to fight. I like people who are willing to stand up for what is right.

181

Not long ago we were planning a special Sunday at our church. Our young people were out visiting and inviting people to come. Somebody called me up and threatened to call the police! I said, "Go ahead." I like it when our young people have the testimony that they're giving the Gospel to people. We're in a battle, and we need to have the testimony that we're fighting for the Lord.

Dr. John R. Rice used to say, "Everybody wants to be in the army of the Lord; they just all want to be in the quartermaster corps." When you became a Christian, you became a soldier, and God expects His army to fight. It's not an army for parades and dress reviews; it's an army to do battle with the enemy, even if he is a giant.

2. Concerned With the Task of the Almighty

David recognized that the primary focus of what was going on was not on him. It was not just about his getting the rewards Saul had offered to the man who fought Goliath. It was not just about Goliath's getting his just deserts for taunting the army of God. That was all part of the battle, but there was something much bigger involved—it was all about God.

> *The battles that you face are an opportunity for God to be honored and glorified in your life.*

The battles you face are an opportunity for God to be honored and glorified in your life. When you face trials and adversity with faith, others see God in a positive light. God has called you to be an overcomer. He does not leave you powerless in the battle. Too many Christians are trying to fight on their own. That is never God's plan.

Do you remember the meeting that Joshua had with the angel of the Lord just before the battle of Jericho? Joshua asked whose side he was on, and the angel replied, "As captain of the host of the LORD am I now come" (Josh. 5:14). David did not go into battle alone, and you don't have to either. God is willing and able to fight on your behalf. Whatever giant is in your life, you can be the victor through His power.

3. Convinced of the Victory

There was no uncertainty in David's mind as to the outcome of the battle. "David said moreover, The LORD that delivered me out of the paw of the lion, and out of the paw of the bear, he will deliver me out of the hand of this Philistine" (I Sam. 17:37). The possibility that Goliath would kill him never even entered David's mind.

David was convinced because of his past. He had seen God work on his behalf before to give him the victory over other enemies. When he was just a boy tending his father's sheep, David had killed a bear and a lion who were threatening the flock. When you look back at the way God has helped you before, it should build and strengthen your faith to trust Him for today's battles.

David was convinced because of God's power. David knew that it was not his own strength that won his battles. He gave the credit to God. His expression of faith that God could overcome any obstacle or enemy was in marked contrast to Saul and the army of Israel. Their view of God was small; David's was large. Never forgot that God Almighty is on your side.

> *When you look at how God has helped you in the past, it should build and strengthen your faith to trust Him for today's battles.*

4. Committed to the Battle

David was not hesitant about his decision to fight. The Bible says, "David hastened, and ran toward the army to meet the Philistine" (I Sam. 17:48). He knew that there was only one true God, and he recognized that the battle with Goliath was an opportunity to demonstrate that truth to every one who witnessed the battle, both Israelites and Philistines.

Halfhearted soldiers do not win battles. History is filled with examples of smaller, less well-equipped armies that defeated superior enemies. During the Revolutionary War, the Continental Army never had the number of men nor the weapons available to the British. But many of the British units were mercenaries fighting for money, while the Americans were fighting for their home and freedom.

During the dark days of World War II, Winston Churchill encouraged his countrymen to continue the fight. He said, "We shall fight on the beaches. We shall fight on the landing grounds. We shall fight in the fields and in the streets. We shall fight in the hills. We shall never surrender!" That is the kind of commitment that wins battles.

5. Conquering the Enemy

When the battle was over, there was no question about who had won. He didn't win on points or a by a TKO. David not only killed Goliath, he cut off his head so there would be no doubt in anyone's mind. God wants you to win the victory completely and thoroughly over every giant in your life.

I heard about a man who wanted to work as a scout for Bear Bryant at the University of Alabama. Another scout was training him and giving him advice. The older man said, "If you go to a high school game and see a player who gets knocked down and doesn't get up again, that's not the guy we want on our team. If you see a guy who gets knocked down and gets back up, but then gets knocked down and stays down, that's not the guy we want either."

Then he said, "If you see a player who gets knocked down and keeps getting back up no matter how many times he gets knocked down..." At that point the young scout interrupted and said, "That's the guy we want!" The old scout said, "No. We want the guy who keeps knocking everybody down!" With God's help and God's power, that can be you! You can win the battles in your Christian life.

The Bible doesn't put the church of Jesus Christ on the defensive. Jesus said, "The gates of hell shall not prevail against it" (Matt. 16:18). That means we are to be attacking the enemy. Go toward the giants in your life in faith. You don't have to "hold on till Jesus comes." "We are more than conquerors through him that loved us" (Rom. 8:37). Take the battle to the enemy and defeat the giants in your life.

Almost three hundred years ago, the great hymn writer Isaac Watts penned these words. Let them be your song as you go into battle to conquer the giants that come against you.

> Am I a soldier of the cross,
>   A follow'r of the Lamb,
> And shall I fear to own his cause
>   Or blush to speak His name?
>
> Must I be carried to the skies
>   On flow'ry beds of ease,
> While others fought to win the prize
>   And sailed through bloody seas?
>
> Are there no foes for me to face?
>   Must I not stem the flood?
> Is this vile world a friend to grace
>   To help me on to God?
>
> Sure, I must fight, if I would reign;

Increase my courage, Lord.
I'll bear the toil, endure the pain,
Supported by Thy Word.

Thy saints in all this glorious war
Shall conquer, though they die.
They see the triumph from afar
And seize it with their eye.

When that illustrious day shall rise
And all Thy armies shine
In robes of victory thro' the skies,
The glory shall be Thine.

For a complete list of available books, write to:
Sword of the Lord Publishers
P. O. Box 1099
Murfreesboro, Tennessee 37133.

(800) 251-4100
(615) 893-6700
FAX (615) 848-6943
www.swordofthelord.com